KINGDOM OF HAPPINESS

Praise for Kingdom of Happiness . . .

This is a guidebook for real happiness that is much-needed in our modern world of division and loneliness. Filled with personal stories about people Fr. Jeffrey Kirby has encountered, it contains concrete steps to building a virtuous life of deep fulfillment and real joy. Fr. Jeffrey Kirby's book will empower the people blessed to read it.

—Representative Paul Ryan
Speaker of the House of Representatives

In Kingdom of Happiness Father Jeffrey Kirby focuses on Jesus' own description of "Happiness" ... He unravels these eight descriptions of happiness by Jesus in a creative, captivating, and inspiring way that will help the reader understand this core message of Jesus' teaching and apply it to his or her own life. This is a great material for anyone's meditation.

—Most Reverend Robert Baker, S.T.D., D.D.
Bishop of Birmingham

I'm undoubtedly biased, because he writes for Crux, but for my money Fr. Jeffrey Kirby is flat-out one of the best spiritual writers going in the Catholic Church today. He's lucid, he's deeply erudite yet writes with a common touch, he's balanced and just utterly "Catholic." I can't recommend his work enough, and I know my own faith has been enriched by it.

—John Allen
President/CEO of Crux Catholic Media, Inc.

Father Jeff Kirby's latest work "Kingdom of Happiness" brings together for me many personal experiences as a pastor and parish priest. As we read this book I pray that the words of a Nigerian Archbishop, which Father Kirby quotes, takes root in our own lives: "God is in Africa because God goes where he is wanted!" I pray that our reading of, and reflection on this work may help us to say that indeed God is wanted in our lives!

—Most Reverend Kevin Vann, J.C.D., D.D.
Bishop of Orange

Understanding the goal of life, the purpose for which God created life—happiness with God for eternity—is the basis for our duty to protect and defend all human life. Father Kirby's book provides us with a way to understand that happiness by showing how the beatitudes define true happiness, summarize "the Law and the Prophets," and give us a measure by which to judge how close we are to the happiness that God has promised... Together with Bible reading and family prayer, Father Kirby's book would be an effective way for families to integrate into their homes their Christian commitment into the Sacramental, particularly Eucharistic, life they live in their parishes.

—Most Reverend Vincenzo Paglia, D.D.
President of the Pontifical Academy of Life

Father Kirby has reflected well on the spiritual value of the Beatitudes. In a way, these statements of Jesus are a "roadmap" for the journey of life and taking them seriously will help those on the journey.

—Most Reverend Robert Guglielmone, D.D.
Bishop of Charleston

Cover and interior design by Caroline Kiser

Cover image: Mountain valley during sunrise / biletskiy / shutterstock.com

Library of Congress Control Number: 2017951203

ISBN: 978-1-5051-0590-2

Published in the United States by

Saint Benedict Press
PO Box 410487
Charlotte, NC 28241
www.SaintBenedictPress.com

Printed and bound in the United States of America

KINGDOM
OF
HAPPINESS

Living the Beatitudes in Everyday Life

Fr. Jeffrey Kirby, STD

SAINT BENEDICT ✝ PRESS

Charlotte, North Carolina

To Father V. Walsh, OCSO,
Friend and Mentor

Contents

A Note to the Reader

First Step

Thank you for picking up this book! As you open it, you've already taken the hardest step along a path that could lead you to true happiness. Here's some more good news:

- ## You're not alone.

  Happiness is desired by every human being. Our whole selves, body and soul, are wired for happiness. No one hopes to be miserable, melancholic, confused, or lost. We all want to be happy, preferably with other people, especially those we love and care about. Everyone wants the happiness you want.

- ## There's a way out of misery.

  If you're finding that life lacks meaning or purpose, if it seems that you're always in some form of anguish or anxiety, if happiness appears to have been a childhood fantasy that's a pipedream in an adult world, there is hope. Happiness is possible. It won't be easy. It will require some work, but there is a way that leads to perpetual happiness no matter what this world throws at you.

- *Happiness is a decision.*

  It's true. While not always a comfortable one, happiness is a real, blood and guts, in-the-trenches-of-life decision. It isn't just getting what we want or having everything exactly as we desire it, nor is it just some type of euphoria or emotional high. It's not found in the raw consumption of passing pleasures or the aggressive assertion of self-interests. While these might at times be enjoyable and give some security, they never last and always leave us wanting more.

  Surrounded by so many passing enjoyments, happiness stands out as a choice. We have to choose to be happy. In the midst of our struggles and consolations—the ups and downs of life—we can choose the constant and steady path of happiness. It *is* available to us.

- *Someone else does the heavy lifting.*

  It might seem too good to be true, but it's not. Someone else is willing to do the heavy lifting of our decision to be happy. Jesus wants to take on the weight of our decision so that he can show us the path to happiness.

  Now bear with me and please don't put the book down. Honestly, I'm not sure what that previous statement about Jesus means to you. I know that some well-intentioned but mistaken people have turned the Gospel into a shallow self-help guidebook, or into some removed, idealistic collection of unhelpful, perhaps condescending, maxims about life, misery, and suffering.

This book will tear down those incomplete or false views of what Jesus Christ wants to do for you and the happiness he wants to share with you. The Lord enters into the trenches of human life as he desires to be with each of us. He offers to help us carry the crosses of our lives so that we can continue to choose to be happy and live a life of uninterrupted happiness.

- *Happiness is a kingdom.*

As we pursue happiness, we'll learn where to find its source. In our decision for happiness, we'll find a way of life and a kingdom born of those who fight to live this way of life. This kingdom is of the spirit, but it can be felt, seen, lived, and shared with others right here and now.

- *The kingdom of happiness can be seen.*

The kingdom that gives true happiness is visible. Yes, we can actually point it out and know its presence. This is possible because it's summarized by principles of discernment and signposts of encouragement called the Beatitudes. These simple markers show us what the kingdom of happiness is, how we can recognize it, and how we know when we are living within it.

Conversion to Happiness

Some years ago, I was the director of a Catholic residence for men. The house consisted of young adult men in graduate studies or in the early part of their professional careers who wanted the Faith to be a part of their lives. It was a great opportunity for them (and me) to grow in prayer, virtue, and selfless service. Many men passed through the house during the years I lived there. To each one, in his own way, I sought to be a spiritual coach and shepherd.

One young man who lived in the house was a convert to Catholicism. In the course of getting to know him, I learned many things about his life, interests, and hopes for the future. In one conversation, I asked him, "What did you convert from?" Without skipping a beat, and with a huge smile on his face, he responded, "Unhappiness, Father. I left a lot of unhappiness and found something greater!" I was surprised. I was expecting the name of some other religious tradition, but this young man went to the heart of the matter. In knowing about the sufferings and heartaches of his life, I knew there had been a lot of previous unhappiness and a lot of reasons that could have led him to choose anger, resentment, and self-pity.

In spite of all these darker possibilities, which so many people choose in our world today, this person chose to convert to happiness. It wasn't a walk in the park for him. He had to fight to persevere in his decision, but he was willing to do it. He saw the choice between light and dark, life and death, happiness and misery, and he chose—without question—to be happy.

In our lives, we have to make our own choice. Will it be an unending and frustrating search for the pleasures and highs of life? Or will we break free from the malaise of incomplete joys and passing pleasures?

A Second Step

As you started reading this book, I mentioned that you've already taken the hardest step along a path that could lead you to true happiness. Therefore, I'd like to ask you to take a second step and continue reading this book so that you might encounter the kingdom of happiness described through the Beatitudes. As you begin to see this kingdom sitting on the horizon, remember that citizenship within its walls is available *right now*. You are welcome at all times.

The choice is yours. Will you choose happiness?

The Choice Between Two Kingdoms

*Enter by the narrow gate; for the gate is wide
and the way is easy, that leads to destruction,
and those who enter by it are many. For the
gate is narrow and the way is hard, that leads
to life, and those who find it are few.*

MATTHEW 7:13–14

Our Decision

Some years ago, a young woman came to see me. This particular woman was always flawlessly dressed—easily turning heads—and seemed to enjoy the attention that came with her beauty. Generally speaking, she appeared content, and so I wasn't sure why she wanted to see a priest.

When the appointment came, she walked into my office, sat down, and within seconds began to sob uncontrollably. In my head, I ran quickly through a list of possible hardships she could've been facing, but I obviously didn't know what was wrong.

When she regained some composure, she looked up at me—her makeup smeared, her nose running—and said, "He proposed!" And then she began to weep again. At this point, I was very confused. Proposed? That sounds like something good, right?

Eventually, the young woman told me the whole story. She had a boyfriend; they had dated for some time, and now he had proposed to her. "He really loves me," she said. "He wants me to be with him forever."

It seemed like this should be a cause for joy, yet the woman was terrified. All her life, she had used her beauty to manipulate and trick people, even her own father, who she often charmed and kept under her control. Her beauty was a source of power that always got her what she wanted. People were pawns and love was a distant reality.

Now her boyfriend had proposed, and her power was threatened. In the proposal, a man was saying to her, "I love you. I love you without ulterior motive, without self-ishness, without counting the cost. I love you for your sake alone." It was a true expression of love, a real poverty of spirit with all the vulnerability and uncertainty that comes with it. And it rocked the plastic, artificial world of this vain, self-absorbed woman. She was sincerely confused and felt totally lost.

After she shared her story and I delivered some initial pastoral counseling, I outlined everything she had shared with me and explained that she had a choice: "Will you choose to accept and return this love? Will you choose happiness?"

These questions belong not only to this young woman but to each of us. In our lives, which can become so crowded, conditioned, and confusing, will we choose to break through all that seeks to entangle us and choose a way of life that will bring us happiness?

This decision is the deal maker or the deal breaker on whether happiness will become a reality in our lives.

Happiness and Freedom

As the option of choosing happiness is presented to us, it's important to understand the nature of freedom. A proper understanding of freedom is at the heart of happiness. Contrary to the lifeless machinery of the Wall Street, Hollywood, Madison Avenue, and Washington, DC, cultures, happiness is not found in money, appearances, material possessions, or power. In summary, happiness does not rely on the state of affairs of this world. We have a power given to us, a power to find grace within our fallen world and transcend it. This power is freedom.

As St. Paul teaches, "For freedom Christ has set us free" (Gal 5:1). That's not the end of that scriptural passage, but let's return to it in a moment.

In the arenas of our culture today, freedom is an abused, poorly taught, or incompletely defined concept. For some, freedom is a fantasy. They think, *If I could just have this one thing* (perhaps winning the lottery), *I'd be free to live as I want.* This concept of freedom doesn't mean anything because those in this situation feel stuck or vanquished by some spiritual trouble or material obstacle, and that one thing they want will not assuage these underlying issues. For others, freedom is simply a license to do whatever they want. Such people perceive no limit to the fulfillment of their desires, however destructive or self-centered those desires are.

Contrary to cultural currents and the sentiments of many, these understandings do not truthfully or holistically define freedom. Rather than a fantasy or a license to do whatever we please, true freedom comes when our lives are ordered toward friendship with God. When we choose goodness, freedom flows within our souls like blood through our hearts.

One married man may think he is free because he can meet his mistress on a Friday night and no one can stop him while his neighbor, a faithful husband, is not free because he feels bound by his marriage vows. But the adulterous husband becomes a slave to his decisions as he sneaks around, constantly afraid that he will be caught. Even if he denies it, his soul is weighed down by remorse. Conversely, the faithful husband lives with true freedom because he knows his life is being ordered toward goodness, toward a faithful marriage and God. He has nothing to hide and lives in the bliss of this reality.

Yes, we are free to do what we like, just like that man may choose to cheat on his wife, but our freedom is perfected by choosing the good. The *Catechism of the Catholic Church* says, "Freedom is the power, rooted in reason and will, to act or not to act, to do this or that, and so to perform deliberate actions on one's own responsibility. By free will one shapes one's own life. Human freedom is a force for growth and maturity in truth in goodness; it attains its perfection when directed toward God, our beatitude" (CCC 1731).

So, at its core, freedom is the power to choose between two things, but our freedom is strengthened when we do what is right, when we choose goodness in the midst of wickedness, truth in a world of error, and real beauty in a culture of ugliness. Freedom helps us to know that sin doesn't define us, tragedy does not have to overwhelm us, and disappointment or confusion do not have to embitter us. We are free and we have the power to choose.

At the funeral service of Senator Clementa Pinckney, the pastor who was killed in a mass shooting during a Bible study at the Mother Emanuel AME Church in Charleston, South Carolina, a close friend of the late senator recounted their friendship. He said the two spoke almost every day and, after the shooting, there were times when he would pick up his phone to talk with his friend before remembering that he was dead and he would feel great sorrow and anguish. But then he would catch himself, smile, and say, "I will not let yesterday's sorrow steal today's joy."

We have a choice. Life can be hard, disillusioning, and tempting. There are the loss of loved ones, financial struggles, health concerns, family or relationship problems, moral difficulties, and an array of other problems. But life can also be joyful, full of meaning and purpose, and a source of encouragement. Who or what determines which path we will follow? Not the ways of this world or merely our emotions; rather, we do. We're free, and we can choose to be happy by ordering our lives toward friendship with God.

And so let's give the full quote from St. Paul: "For freedom Christ has set us free; stand fast therefore, and do not submit again to a yoke of slavery" (Gal 5:1). Paul is telling us that we don't have to be slaves in the kingdom of men; we have the freedom to find a new kingdom.

Happiness and Suffering

In knowing of our freedom to choose happiness, we have to state the obvious. Happiness is not found solely in pleasure, ease, or comfort. It's not temporary euphoria or an isolated sense of self-fulfillment. If we bounce along a series of pleasures, skipping from one enjoyable sensation to another and living in make-believe realities, we will find ourselves living under that yoke of slavery St. Paul just warned us about.

It's similar to a drug or sex addict who lives a shallow life in between the momentary highs of his addiction. In such a scenario, life becomes all about us. Such a slavery is not happiness but a type of existential tyranny of euphoria. Such people trick themselves into believing they are happy with each new high, no matter what they feel during the lows.

But it isn't just the addicts who live a counterfeit sense of happiness. Many of us have no inclination to drug or alcohol abuse, and yet we live as if life was a theatrical performance. Everyone is either given or assumed to have an assigned role, script, and stage cues. Nothing is real and everything revolves around unbridled narcissism. Think no further than the nature of social media, where we put up a front of ourselves that is often far from the real thing. This fabricated happiness is no happiness at all.

How can anyone think happiness is possible in either fragile situation when we approach life like the addict or the stage actor? How could we allow our happiness to be tethered to the uncertainty of euphoria or the conditions of a counterfeit world?

Ironically, it is often the other extremes of life that bring about true happiness; not the false highs the world can provide us through so many different means, but rather the suffering we encounter.

In choosing to be happy, we must accept suffering. Some believe that suffering destroys our chance at happiness, but when it's accepted in the right spirit, suffering purifies and intensifies happiness. We're all willing to suffer for what we love; a priest is willing to accept hardship for his parish, spouses for one another, parents for their children, leaders for those in their charge, and good citizens for the causes of justice and peace.

It may be difficult to hear, but suffering is a prerequisite to happiness in a fallen world. We must be willing to suffer, to truly die to ourselves, our passions, our self-centeredness, our sense of justice, our desire for comfort and ease, and our perception of what the world should be in order to truly find and live in the kingdom of happiness. Properly understood, suffering can be an enduring teacher, a tempered comforter, and a source of perseverance along the way to happiness.

Our human experience provides us with a full panorama of examples that convey this truth. Think about:

- The husband and father who is terminally ill, suffering from his medical treatments and knowing that he will leave his family soon, and yet is joyful because he knows that he has *today* with his family, that heaven is real, and that he has the opportunity to show his children how to live and die with grace.

- The single mother who works two jobs, suffers from standing on her feet throughout the day, barely makes ends meet, has no support, and yet is joyful because she's doing it all for her kids.

- The husband who has to work late each night to support his family but prays hard for the energy and will he needs to not only provide for his family but be there for them as well, and finds happiness knowing his labors are a necessary part of life but don't have to rob him of family joys.

- The young adult who loses friends and becomes an outcast because he chooses not to partake in certain thrills and frivolities, and yet is happy because of the knowledge that his good choices will bring about true friends in the future.

- The reader of this book. What is your experience? What has overtaken your soul and robbed you of your happiness?

Defining Happiness

Now that we know we have a conscious choice to be happy and have properly explained the true nature of freedom and the role suffering can play in our happiness, let's try to pin down what exactly happiness is.

As we've already seen, the definition of happiness is essential; it provides us with a solid foundation. If a man chiefly values the pursuit of great wealth, then when his fortune is taken away (as it often will be in one way or another), he will fall into a state of despair. But here is the key: the financial trouble itself isn't the source of his despair; it was his false definition of happiness. His foundation was weak from the get-go.

With this noted, then, what is happiness?

Biblically speaking, it's receiving, accepting, and seeking to live in a state of beatitude, a condition of being blessed. Some might not know that this is literally what the word beatitude means—"blessed." Happiness is the satisfaction that comes from this beatitude and the awareness of this blessing and its providence, power, and purpose in our lives.

While there are numerous examples of a blessing being given in Sacred Scripture, from Shem being blessed by Noah, Abraham blessing Isaac, Israel's blessing of Judah, and so on, all human blessings are an expression of the singular blessing given by God to humanity. This blessing began at the creation of the heavens and the earth, but it spans salvation history and culminates in Jesus Christ, who is *the* Beatitude—*the* Blessing—and therefore *the* Happiness of God.

When we begin to see Jesus as the Happiness of God, I'm hoping new doors will open in our hearts. Since so many people have hijacked or disfigured the person of the Lord Jesus, it's good to approach him in his principal place, which biblically is expressed as "the right hand of God" (Acts 7:55–56). This is a place of privilege, favor, and blessing. The Lord Jesus dwells and basks in his eternal identity as the "delight" of God as we read in the Book of Proverbs (8:30–31). In this light, we should begin to understand why the Lord has come to us, why he has broken through every misery, sin, tragedy, heartache, and suffering in order to be with us.

The Lord came to share the beatitude the blessing with us when he came to share himself. Though it may not be the same sort of fabricated happiness the world offers us, he wants us to be happy and partake and relish in his kingdom of happiness.

The Lord's invitation is not a distant or foreign one. Jesus Christ did not fall from the sky or emerge as a superhero. He came as one of us. He was born to a mother, lived in a family, loved others, shared in hard work, laughed among friends, cried and felt sorrow, was rejected by those he cared about, understood poverty, was falsely accused of evil, tortured, and

died. The Lord Jesus lived a fully human life. He experienced
such a life in order to show us how to live, how to suffer, and
how to rejoice.

The Lord's life was not easy, or comfortable, but he perse-
vered in his happiness because his actions were always ordered
toward the good, toward friendship with God. Jesus did not
promise the same kind of happiness the world claims to give
us, in fact, he told us that we, too, would have to carry our
cross (see Mt 16:24), but if we carry this cross with sacrificial
joy, as he did, we will share in the richness of his happiness.

But we have to accept his call to pick up our cross. Yes,
our call for happiness is not an empty decision floating in the
cosmos, or a misplaced overconfidence in ourselves. In choosing to be happy, we must choose Jesus Christ and *his* cross. We
must choose his kingdom. If we do make this choice, we will
give our permission for God's grace to work within us and
bring salvation into our lives.

So will we choose a life of misery, marked by either occa-
sional moments of euphoria or of fabricated realities, or will
we choose a life of authentic, in-the-trenches happiness with
the risen Christ? These are the options: misery or happiness.
What will we choose?

The Way

Jesus tells us that he is "the way, the truth, and the life" (Jn
14:6), and so in him, we can find the map, path, and guide-
posts for our journey to happiness.

From the Lord's own witness and ministry, several marks
of his interior life can be discerned to guide us along the path
to happiness. Jesus listed these marks in his Sermon on the

Mount (Mt 5–7); they are traditionally called the Beatitudes. Truly, Jesus Christ—the Beatitude of God—has given us these steps, or counsels, to help us to live out our decision for happiness.

The remainder of this book will be an exploration of these Beatitudes so that we can see how they validate, sustain, and nurture our desire for happiness. We'll show them being lived out in Scripture and in everyday life, as well as examine their fascinating connections to the gifts of the Holy Spirit, the virtues of the Christian tradition, the petitions of the Lord's Prayer, and the deadly sins (which for our purposes we may call the "anti-beatitudes").

At the close of each chapter, you will see a kind of "spiritual matrix" unfold before your eyes, found in a section called the "School of Discipleship." This matrix, or chart, outlines a web of connections that link the central tenets of the spiritual life. For the purposes of our "School of Discipleship," we will call these "Subjects."

To help you better understand these "Subjects," brief information about each one has been given here. Read it now and refer back to it, if needed, throughout the book.

School of Discipleship "Subjects"

Christian Virtues: The *Catechism of the Catholic Church* defines virtue as "an habitual and firm disposition to do the good. It allows the person not only to perform good acts, but to give the best of himself. The virtuous person tends toward the good with all his sensory and spiritual powers; he pursues the good and chooses it in concrete actions" (CCC 1803). St.

Gregory of Nyssa, in his *De beatitudinibus*, says, "The goal of a virtuous life is to become like God." The *Catechism* names seven Christian, or "heavenly," virtues, broken up into two categories. The four cardinal virtues are prudence, justice, temperance, and courage, while the three theological virtues are faith, hope, and charity (see CCC 1804–29).

Gifts of the Holy Spirit: The *Catechism* tells us that "the moral life of Christians is sustained by the gifts of the Holy Spirit. These are permanent dispositions which make man docile in following the promptings of the Holy Spirit. . . . They belong in their fullness to Christ, Son of David. They complete and perfect the virtues of those who receive them" (CCC 1830–31). In short, these are exactly what they sound like—generous gifts from the Third Person of the Holy Trinity, which he bestows upon us at the will of the Father. They allow us to become better and more virtuous people and overcome the pitfalls of the deadly sins. The seven gifts of the Holy Spirit are wisdom, understanding, counsel, fortitude, knowledge, piety, and fear of the Lord (sometimes referred to as "wonder" or "awe").

Petitions of the Lord's Prayer: Though we may not always consciously realize it, the Lord's Prayer is a series of petitions, or requests, that we make to God. This prayer was given to us by Jesus during his Sermon on the Mount (see Mt 6:5–13), which of course was also when he preached about the

Beatitudes. These seven petitions, outlined in depth in the *Catechism* (2803–54), follow the initial greeting we make, "Our Father, who art in heaven." After this greeting, we ask that God's name be hallowed (honored), that his kingdom comes, that his will be done, that we be given our daily bread, that we be forgiven our trespasses, that we not be led into temptation, and that we be delivered from evil. Moving forward, we will see how each of the Beatitudes is a "blossoming" of these petitions.

Seven Deadly Sins ("Anti-Beatitudes"): The *Catechism* defines sin as "an offense against reason, truth, and right conscience; it is failure in genuine love for God and neighbor caused by a perverse attachment to certain goods. It wounds the nature of man and injures human solidarity" (CCC 1849). Though there are many different sorts of sins, the Church and her tradition classifies them in a list of seven "capital" or "deadly" sins. Each transgression we commit can be traced back to pride, avarice (greed), envy, wrath, lust, gluttony, and sloth (see CCC 1866). For our purposes, in showing them as a contrast to the Beatitudes, we may refer to them as the "anti-beatitudes."

Note: As you read through the explanations and study the chart, remember that we are drawing all these things back to the Beatitudes, not necessarily drawing parallels between the "Subjects" themselves. While the Christian tradition does have a history of showing the interconnectedness of these aspects of the spiritual life, our work is focused on their relationship to the Beatitudes. Additionally, all explanations are kept brief to simply graze the surface of this rich theology. For any reader who wishes to go deeper, see the bibliography for resources that can provide more detail.

CHAPTER 1

POOR IN SPIRIT

*Blessed are the poor in spirit, for
theirs is the kingdom of heaven.*

MATTHEW 5:3

God Goes Where He Is Wanted!

When I was in the seminary, I had the unique opportunity
to spend some time in Imo State, Nigeria. One of the local
archbishops, a friend of my diocese, invited and hosted me
for the visit. In my time there, I was able to see the vibrant
faith of the people reflected in beautiful masses, inspirational
singing, the people's love for their shepherds, the building of
hospitals and churches by the hands of the faithful, and by an
intense and warm sense of welcome. I had never experienced
the Christian faith in such a profoundly encouraging way.

During my stay, the archbishop made time for me every
evening to discuss what I had seen or learned. As my time in
Nigeria came to a close, he asked me, "Jeffrey, why is God in
Africa?" I was confused by the question, unsure of what he
was looking for. My face must have shown my bewilderment
because the archbishop asked me again in a slightly raised

1

voice, "Jeffrey, why is God in Africa?" I finally responded, "I don't know, Your Grace."

The high churchman sat back in his chair with a broad smile and a cheerful smirk. He paused, then quickly sat forward, looked me directly in the eyes, and said, "Jeffrey, God is in Africa because God goes where he is wanted!"

It was a powerful moment for me and the catalyst for a great leap forward in my own discipleship. The archbishop was correct in noting the massive growth of the Catholic Church in Africa. He knew this was happening because of their fidelity to the truths of faith and the moral life flowing from it. They had also enacted wide-ranging social outreach and educational endeavors for the betterment of all peoples (Christian and non-Christian). There was immense happiness in the African community despite very real suffering, poverty, and hardships.

By every popular Western standard, the Christian disciples in Africa have no reason to be happy; in fact, they have every possible reason *not* to want God and even feel betrayed by him. From diseases, government corruption, gangs and abuse, human trafficking, drug trades, mass murders, foreign monopolies of natural resources, unemployment, religious extremism and terrorism, domestic violence, and multiple other evils and social ills, the people of Africa could easily cry "foul" toward God and walk away from any claims to happiness. Many of their Western counterparts, having far fewer sufferings, have already done so and abandoned religious faith.

The decision of these African believers for happiness, however, teaches them that being happy cannot depend on the passing things of this world that are so easily lost. Happiness is not an escape from real life or the construction of a pseudo-heaven that leaves behind struggles and sufferings. With their happiness based firmly on their faith in God, these Christians do not expect leisure or comfort. They can walk boldly through the sorrows of this world and still find joy. They understand that God never promised to remove our sufferings, but in fact promised to help us carry them and redeem us through them. This understanding, and the faith born from it, is where happiness can be legitimately grounded and become a well-spring of hope and inspiration to us and to those around us.

This reliance on God is best understood by the biblical expression "poor in spirit." Just as these Christians in Africa give witness to it, we are all called to be poor in spirit and to depend on God as the "pioneer and perfecter" of our faith (Heb 12:2).

Surrendering to Our Need for God

In our lives and in our own choices, we have to approach the kingdom of happiness with a poverty of spirit. As shown in the lives of so many witnesses, being poor in spirit is not always easy. It can be grueling, but it's the beginning of the path to true, stable, and vibrant happiness.

Poverty of spirit begins with a mutual and parallel acknowledgment of both our need for God as well as his all-powerful blessing and care for us in all things. Being poor in spirit means we choose not to command things of God, our world, loved ones, or of ourselves. We truly surrender and seek to be open to receive all things as a gift from our heavenly Father and to generously give ourselves in service to our neighbors. The decision to be poor in spirit is a choice to live in reverence of God and in detachment to the things of this world. It's both a selection and an election into the kingdom of heaven, which is the kingdom of happiness.

Admittedly, a choice to live dependent on anyone, even God, is immensely counter-cultural in the West today. We are told, pressured, and convinced to rely only on ourselves, to "stand on our own two feet," to refuse help, avoid assistance, and fuel a radical sense of our own autonomy. We are programmed to become what realist philosophers describe as "the sovereign self." This egotism and the pride it fosters wars against our decision to be happy. It's precisely what has to be dethroned in order for us to be truly poor in spirit and begin to recognize and live within the kingdom of happiness.

We see in the life of Jesus Christ an unsurpassed model of poverty in spirit.

St. Paul teaches us, "For you know the grace of our Lord Jesus Christ, that though he was rich, yet for your sake he became poor, so that by his poverty you might become rich" (2 Cor 8:9). In another of his letters, the apostle stresses the Lord Jesus's poverty of spirit by citing a popular Christian hymn of his day: "Have this mind among yourselves, which was in Christ Jesus, who, though he was in the form of God, did not count equality with God a thing to be grasped, but emptied himself, taking the form of a servant, being born in the likeness of men. And being found in human form he humbled himself and became obedient unto death, even death on a cross" (Phil 2:5–8).

This passage is oftentimes called the "kenosis hymn." The word *kenosis* comes from the Greek *ekenosen,* which means "he emptied himself." It beautifully depicts the Lord's own poverty of spirit as he relied on God and lovingly poured himself out for humanity.

As with Jesus, so with each of us. In our desire and search for happiness, we are invited to accompany the Lord Jesus in becoming poor in spirit.

Turning Things Right Side Up

St. Paul is among the great shepherds of the Christian tradition, but this wasn't always so. At one point in his life, he was a persecutor of Christians and even oversaw their deaths. But in the midst of his murderous zeal, the Lord Jesus came to him and rocked Paul's world, inviting the once-persecutor of Christians to become a believer in the Gospel (see Acts 9:1–19). Jesus offered a man who was miserable a chance at happiness. And Paul, bruised, broken, and blind, accepted the invitation.

The Acts of the Apostles recounts the far-reaching ministry of the belated apostle to the Gentiles. On one occasion, St. Paul and his companions traveled to Thessalonica (later he would write two letters to the Christians in this city: 1 and 2 Thessalonians). Upon entering the city, Paul went to the local synagogue and began to preach about Jesus Christ and the resurrection. Many Jewish men, God-fearing Greeks, and prominent women were convinced by his apostolic preaching. Others, however, were jealous of the apostle and the conversions brought about by his ministry. They gathered together a group of some bad characters and started a mob in the marketplace.

But St. Paul and his followers had already left the marketplace and gone to the home of Jason, a recent convert. The mob went to the house, and when they couldn't find the Christian teachers, they dragged Jason out of his home and took him to the local authorities, declaring that the Gospel had turned the world "upside down" and that Jason was giving them hospitality (Acts 17:6–8). Jason had to pay a bond while St. Paul and his group left the city.

It's interesting that the Thessalonians would argue that the Gospel proclamation, which is the message of happiness, would turn the world "upside down." We could argue more legitimately that the Good News actually turns the world *right side up*, since left to our own devices we find only self-centeredness and misery in a world marked by confusion and darkness. While momentary happiness might be possible, true and consistent happiness can only be found in a world that is right side up; that is, facing in a direction beyond itself, toward God, who is all-good and the source of long-lasting happiness.

In highlighting the preaching of the early Church, we should remind ourselves that the life of the apostles and their disciples was not an easy one. St. Paul explains:

> For I think that God has exhibited us apostles as last of all, like men sentenced to death; because we have become a spectacle to the world, to angels and to men. We are fools for Christ's sake, but you are wise in Christ. We are weak, but you are strong. You are held in honor, but we in disrepute. To the present hour we hunger and thirst, we are poorly clothed and buffeted and homeless, and we labor, working with our own hands. When reviled, we bless; when persecuted, we endure; when slandered, we try to conciliate; we have become, and are now, as the refuse of the world, the dregs of all things. (1 Cor 4:9–13)

And in a different letter he continues more emphatically:

> But as servants of God we commend ourselves
> in every way: through great endurance, in afflic-
> tions, hardships, calamities, beatings, imprisonments,
> tumults, labors, watching, hunger; by purity, knowl-
> edge, forbearance, kindness, the Holy Spirit, genuine
> love, truthful speech, and the power of God; with the
> weapons of righteousness for the right hand and for
> the left; in honor and dishonor, in ill repute and good
> repute. We are treated as impostors, and yet are true; as
> unknown, and yet well known; as dying, and behold
> we live; as punished, and yet not killed; as sorrowful,
> yet always rejoicing; as poor, yet making many rich;
> as having nothing, and yet possessing everything. (2
> Cor 6:4–10)

Clearly the apostles and first generation of Christians endured
a hard life. And yet they saw their sufferings as opportunities
to put their world right side up, to be poor in spirit and grow
deeper in their decision for happiness.

Like the Christians in Africa today, the patristic-era
Christians relished in their reliance on God. Will we choose a
similar poverty of spirit?

The Widow's Mile

In his public teachings, the Lord praised an unexpected example of someone living poor in spirit. While in the Temple,
Jesus looked up and saw many rich people putting their gifts
into the treasury. He also observed a poor widow putting in
two mites, the smallest of copper coins valued at a halfpenny.

Most people would have overlooked the widow since her social status was not one of prominence and her gift was not a significant one in terms of monetary value.

The Lord Jesus, however, saw something others did not. "Truly I tell you, this poor widow has put in more than all of them; for they all contributed out of their abundance, but she out of her poverty put in all the living that she had" (Lk 21:3–4). The two mites the woman gave reflected her sustenance and basic well-being. By giving them, she showed her complete dependency on God. She manifested that her life was a living supplication to God and his goodness.

The widow chose a happiness that is not given by this world, one that the proud and self-reliant can never understand.

In our lives, are we in the crowd with those who gave from their abundance, or are we in the company of this holy widow?

Mount to Mission

With each of the Beatitudes, we have to try to understand how we can live them out in our daily lives. We have to take what Jesus taught us on the mount and make it our mission to live out those teachings.

So what is our "mount to mission" strategy for becoming poor in spirit?

As we've seen in the lives of the holy ones, our decision for happiness will bring forth a desire to live with a poverty of spirit. While this is an authentic inclination given to us as children of God, we will feel a battle within our hearts since—although we were created good—we are fallen and crave to possess, own, and control ourselves, things, other people, and even God. This craving is fed by fear, anxiety, constant restlessness, and an insatiable appetite for more.

The battle, however, is worth the fight, and the conflict will have two major fronts: one of the spirit and the other within the material world. Neither should be overemphasized or neglected. The summons to live poor in spirit is not only a spiritual call to dependency and humility but also a command to temperance and detachment.

In his teachings, Jesus never promised health or wealth. Those who preach such a message are false prophets who adulterate the Gospel and obscure the path to heaven. It is important for us to know what the Lord promised and the life he invites us to live so that we can be happy.

As we seek to follow the real Gospel—the Gospel that shows us the meaning and value of suffering and poverty— God is able to sustain our happiness and bless us with freedom, flexibility, and a forgiving spirit.

In receiving these blessings, we will actively seek a poverty of spirit in all the material and spiritual areas of our lives. This includes how we approach abilities and talents, our health, our aging process and limitations, the future, our prestige, the affection of others, time, accepting correction, giving guidance, and how we own and use the things of this world.

Some general examples of how others have owned or used things in a desire to live a simplicity of life include:

- The person who is going to buy another pair of shoes but then considers their closet's current supply, chooses not to purchase the shoes, and instead buys a pair for someone with a greater need in their community.

- A married couple using Natural Family Planning who

welcomes God's gift of new life and all its challenges, while also, at times, practicing chastity at the expense of their physical desires.

- The older woman who struggles from despair about her declining appearance but ultimately accepts the reality of aging and welcomes the blessings that come with growing older, offering to watch her grandchildren one night so that her daughter and son-in-law can take a date night.

- The young man making millions for a large bank who gives up his life of luxury to start a charity helping impoverished youth.

- The teenager who shops at local thrift stores and will wear any clean and decent clothes and is not worried about name brands and the vanity games of his or her peers.

In living with a poverty of spirit, we are able to exercise virtue, especially temperance in our daily actions and charity to those in need.

Additionally, the desire to pray is enhanced and intensified within our souls as we realize our deep need for God and our dependence on him. Lastly, as we live a life poor in spirit, we have nothing to lose as we seek to advocate for justice and peace. We are empowered to speak the truth in love and to undergo any persecution for the sake of goodness and beauty.

An Examination of Conscience

- Do I acknowledge that my happiness comes from God and his blessings?

- Do I let myself fully understand how greatly I need God and his grace in my life?

- Do I actively participate in Mass and seek ways to revere God and his majesty?

- Am I ungrateful to God and those around me?

- Do I blame situations or other people for my misery?

- Do I accept sufferings as opportunities to mature and deepen in my desire for happiness?

- Do I believe myself to be better than or superior to others?

- Do I engage in flattery or gossip?

- Do I overspend, live beyond my means, cheat others, or live in a needlessly frugal way with myself or others?

- Am I temperate in my use of food, alcohol, medication, and the treatment of my body or the body of another?

School of Discipleship

As we mentioned in the introduction, this section, found at the conclusion of each chapter, will outline a series of fascinating links between the Beatitudes and the Christian virtues, the gifts of the Holy Spirit, the petitions of the Lord's Prayer, and the deadly sins (or anti-beatitudes).

Through the unfolding of this chart and its corresponding explanations, you'll see how all these aspects of the spiritual life point back, in a myriad of ways, to the blessings of the Beatitudes. These connections are no coincidence, but rather a testament to the balance and harmony of Christ's teachings.

This fascinating chart will thus provide you with a roadmap to find the kingdom of happiness.

With this in mind, let's look at the first beatitude: **poor in spirit**.

As we grow in spiritual poverty, the Holy Spirit bestows on us the gift of **fear of the Lord**, sometimes called "awe" or "wonder." A person with wonder and awe knows that God is the perfection of all we desire. This gift guides us in seeing God's glory and his work in our lives. We can see how this goes hand in hand with a poverty of spirit since such a state helps us acknowledge our need for God (acknowledging our need for him leads to an "awe" of him).

Once we receive this gift, the virtue of **temperance** is perfected in our soul, which is properly using the created things of the world according to the purpose for which they have been given. It is knowing how to put "first things first"; namely, putting God first and putting our own wants and desires second. More common terms would be moderation or self-control. If we keep a poverty of spirit and if we fear the Lord, we will refrain from wanting and asking for too much, because we will know we should only want whatever God sends us, and no more.

This beatitude, gift, and virtue help us to better understand the petition in the Lord's Prayer **"hallowed be thy name"** since in this utterance we acknowledge God's majesty and our lowliness before him. The blossoming of this petition leads us to the promise of this beatitude, which is to inherit the kingdom of heaven. If we honor God and his name, we will become his adopted sons and daughters and have a share in his inheritance.

Lastly, the path that begins from this beatitude and crosses through these other aspects of the spiritual life helps us over-come the capital sin of **pride**. It should be clear how an inflated sense of self keeps us from being poor in spirit, as well as from fearing the Lord and keeping his name "hallowed." Pride is a rebellion against God in order to serve ourselves, and in doing so, we lack temperance because we have made the decision to put ourselves first. With pride, we fail to have dependency and trust and seek to take in as much glory as we can for ourselves. The dark spirit of pride creates a small world that revolves only around us, our talents, our perceived power, and the use of things and other people as a means for our own use and enjoyment. This is the sin of the fallen angels, of our first parents, and of every soul doomed to per-dition. And for many, it can be a hell on earth.

As the promise of the poor in spirit is the kingdom of heaven, so the punishment of the anti-beatitude is this small, suffocating world full of loneliness and emptiness.

In conclusion, the first row of our spiritual matrix looks like this:

BEATITUDE	GIFT OF THE SPIRIT	CORRESPONDING VIRTUE	PETITION OF THE LORD'S PRAYER	CAPITAL SIN/ ANTI-BEATITUDE
Blessed are the poor in spirit, for theirs is the kingdom of heaven	Fear of the Lord	Temperance	Hallowed be thy name	Pride

Prayer

Heavenly Father,
I want to be happy. Keep me from misery and the lies of this world.
As so many things promise happiness, I turn and surrender to you.
I am poor in spirit and desperately need you.
Come to me as I wait, empty and open to your grace.
Nothing can fill me with happiness except you and your blessings.
Bring me into your kingdom! Bless me with happiness!
Through Christ our Lord. Amen.

Three Helpful Truths to Live a Poverty of Spirit:

+ We did not create ourselves.
+ All that we have has been given to us.
+ All that we possess will be taken from us, whether we like it or not.

Promise of the Lord Jesus

Come to me, all who labor and are heavy laden, and I will give you rest. Take my yoke upon you, and learn from me; for I am gentle and lowly in heart, and you will find rest for your souls.

Matthew 11:28–29

Prayer of Job

Naked I came from my mother's womb, and naked shall I return; the Lord gave, and the Lord has taken away; blessed be the name of the Lord.

Job 1:21

— CHAPTER 2 —

THOSE WHO MOURN

Blessed are those who mourn, for
they shall be comforted.

MATTHEW 5:4

Mourning Our Sinfulness

When I was being trained for the priesthood, I came to know a relatively new, dynamic group called the *Comunita Cenacolo*. The name is Italian and means the "Cenacle Community"; it is a reference to the upper room where the Lord celebrated both the Last Supper and where his disciples reconvened and received the Holy Spirit on Pentecost. The community is a very active group that ministers to people with drug and other addictions in various parts of the Church.

While not for every person with an addiction, the group's "school of love" stresses a reliance on the Holy Spirit, which is demonstrated by an intense Eucharistic devotion, hard manual labor, regular prayer times, a low tolerance for self-pity, strict obedience to authority, a heavy emphasis on the common good, and a strong insistence on service before oneself.

In getting to know the group, I was so inspired by them

that I requested to do what's called *l'esperienza,* which is when a person joins one of the houses of the community and lives as a member. All privileges, honors, signs of respect, and non-member designations are suspended during the experience. A person becomes a member of the community, sharing in the same expectations and receiving the same disciplines and corrections.

My experience in the community was very hard physically, as well as humbling spiritually. In becoming a member, however, I could listen and learn from the other members, all of whom had sorrowful and yet consoling stories of conversion. Much of the group wallowed in extreme forms of darkness, deception, and violence. Without question, the fallen world of drug abuse is a place of depravity and deformation.

One man's story is still etched in my mind; I'll call him Dave. He explained that he had slowly entered the drug culture but, once within it, his addiction escalated quickly. In time, all his friends were fellow users and everything was placed within the context of finding money to get drugs. His parents became suspicious and approached him about his behavior in order that they might help him. But he shut them out of his life, lied to them, stole their money, and took advantage of their good will and trust.

On one occasion, when Dave wanted to take his friends on a joy ride, his father attempted to take the keys from him. The two wrestled and the son pushed his father away and stormed out. Dave eventually walked to the local park where he met up with his friends. The group was angry that they didn't have a car and didn't have money for drugs. As their frustration and rage grew, they suddenly heard someone walking into the park. They hid in the bushes, and when the person approached, they pounced on him. They mercilessly beat this innocent stranger with the intention of robbing him.

Except, he wasn't a stranger at all. While wielding punches, Dave realized that the person being beaten was his father, who had gone out in search of his son to make sure he was alright and to bring him home. He tried to stop the others but they were out of control. Much harm was done before he could drag his father away and carry him home.

From there, the father had to go to the emergency room, where he was hospitalized for a broken nose and cheek bone, dislocated jaw, broken collar bone and ribs, and an array of other injuries. Dave told me that this experience filled him with shame. He realized that he had become a stranger to himself and had hit rock bottom. It became clear that he was living in misery, and so he repented of his sins, asking God and his family for help to change his life. This conversion led him to the *Comunita Cenacolo*.

And yet, even after entering the community, his father would not look him in the eyes. He approached his son with caution and fear and noticeably sought ways to avoid him. Dave was in continuous mourning, grieving the sins he had committed against himself and his family. He told me he offered up regular penance and constant prayer that his father would look upon him with warmth and trust again.

Dave suffered for some time, but then once on a visit home, after entering his parent's house, his father walked toward him, smiled, and gave him a welcoming embrace. It seemed to come out of nowhere but was presumably the result of his prayers. Dave said to me, "I don't know why he did it. I didn't deserve it. But I'm so grateful that he forgave me and that he will begin to trust me again."

Here is an example of the consolation promised to those who mourn. This story demonstrates the essential and formative role of mourning along our path to happiness. There are no short cuts or compromises to it, not if we want our happiness to be real and our consolation true. This is the mourning that we must be willing to accept and endure since it purifies, enlightens, and strengthens us against sin and misery, the ancient enemies of happiness.

Redemptive Mourning

If we have entered the kingdom of happiness through a poverty of spirit, we will begin to see how liberating this way of life can be. But at times, the Lord Jesus may still present us with the unenviable and at times freighting dilemma of mourning. We have no control over the heartache and tragedy that might befall us, nor the purgative and sobering truth of mourning. Sometimes we must suffer; it's as simple as that.

But it is our willingness to accept and integrate the lessons of mourning, sorrow, and helplessness that allow us to know who we are, as well as help us comprehend our inescapable reliance on God. The receptive posture nurtured by a spirit of mourning opens our hearts to receive his consolation so that we may persevere along the path to happiness.

To fully understand this beatitude, it is important that we recognize the different types of mourning that exist. Most people turn immediately to the loss of a loved one when they consider their own mourning. While this is not an exclusive definition, it's understandable that people would immediately think of this since it is the acutest form of grief. This particular sorrow over death and the vulnerability it brings can be so profound it can even affect us physically, as people are known to lose weight and sleep as the stress overwhelms them.

But we can also mourn over the state of our fallen world and the reality of our own sins, as we saw in the young man in the *Comunita Cenacolo*. When we reflect on the darkness or maliciousness that we have chosen, and the goodness and beauty that we have declined, our hearts are filled with sorrow and anguish. St. Paul summarizes it perfectly:

> I do not understand my own actions. For I do not do what I want, but I do the very thing I hate. Now if I do what I do not want, I agree that the law is good. So then it is no longer I that do it, but sin which dwells within me. For I know that nothing good dwells with me, that is, in my flesh. I can will what is right, but I cannot do it. For I do not do the good I want, but the evil I do not want is what I do. Now if I do what I do not want, it is no longer I that do it, but sin which dwells within me. . . . Wretched man that I am! Who will deliver me from this body of death? Thanks be to God through Jesus Christ our Lord! So then, I of myself serve the law of God with my mind, but with my flesh I serve the law of sin. (Rom 7:15–20, 24–25)

We should be reminded here of those important words we say at Mass when we ask forgiveness for "what I have done, and what I have failed to do." Each of us has done the evil we do not want to do and have not done the good that we desire to do. St. Paul exclaims, "Who will rescue me?" It is exactly this sense of desperation and the admission of our frailty that allows us to truly mourn the evil we have done and the good we have failed to do.

Let's stop for a moment and point out something very important. Think back to the most common form of mourning we have already discussed: when we grieve over the loss of a loved one. Our anguish is a proof of our love for that person, for we would not mourn someone we did not love. This love is a good thing, so we are mourning the loss of a good. Think now to the mourning of our own sins; this, in a similar sense, is also mourning the loss of a good, because we forfeit God's grace when we sin, and his grace is certainly something good. When we think about it this way, we can see how these two forms of mourning are connected.

But let's return to Dave and focus on his father for a moment, because of course we also mourn the sins (the loss of goodness) of our loved ones. Imagine the older man's internal suffering over the darkness his son was choosing to live in. There is a common expression that goes, "A parent is only as happy as his saddest child." Meaning, a father or mother could have four children living a perfect life, but if just one has gone astray, the parent will suffer greatly. Look no further than the father of the prodigal son as evidence; the faithfulness of his older son did not alleviate the grief he felt as his younger son went and lived a life of sin and debauchery (see Lk 15:11–32).

But it doesn't have to just be our own sins or of those we love that cause us sorrow. If we truly understand God's will and what a life of virtue should look like, then the many sins of the world can devastate us. Think of the tragedies of war and terrorism, the violence of abortion, the redefinition of marriage, drug and alcohol abuse, racism, and the widespread removal of God from the public square. Knowing the goodness and beauty with which God originally created us leads us into mourning as we see the false kingdom of darkness that overshadows the world.

Then there are the many sufferings of the world that lead us into mourning, including natural disasters like hurricanes, fires, earthquakes, and tsunamis, as well as sicknesses like cancer that are beyond our control. We can find ourselves turning to God and asking, "Why is this happening?" as we try to make sense of the shock and sorrow in our souls.

Finding Comfort

But mourning, in all its many forms, can lead us to a deeper understanding of human life and our relationship with God. Christ told us that those who mourn will be "comforted" (Mt 5:4). What exactly does this mean? How are we comforted when we mourn?

In one sense, the comfort we will be rewarded with may not be fully realized until we reach heaven. But even in this life, we can get a sense of the solace Jesus offers us through our times of mourning.

Many people talk about a kind of peace that comes over them after the death of a loved one, knowing they are in a better place. We, of course, mourn their last days in the hospital, their death and funeral, cleaning out their possessions, and handling their affairs. But once that time has passed, we can rejoice over their entry into eternal life and enjoy the many memories we shared with them, appreciating them in a new and profound way. We never enjoy the fact that they are gone, but a sense of understanding and resignation washes over us that quiets our soul.

Or think of the times we suffer physically and emotionally.

We try to fight through the difficult times, thinking we can rely on our own strength, but eventually, we come to the realization that we can do nothing without God. When we reach that point of surrender and accept his will, we are infused with a sense of comfort and peace, knowing things do not depend on our own power and ability. Suffering helps us acknowledge our dependence on him, and anytime we are brought back to him in prayer, we will be rewarded with a kind of inner peace that seemed impossible when the agony began. Not only this, the Lord will send others to us, friends and family, to console us in our times of need.

Consider also when we mourn our sins. When we repent and come to Jesus in the confessional, we are often overcome with profound peace as we walk back out. His mercy brings us the comfort we could never have if we continued a life of sin. And lastly, we can also be comforted when we mourn the fallen state of the world, knowing that we were not created for this broken place, but rather a kingdom that awaits us where sin and pain cannot be found.

In the Gospel according to St. Luke, we're told of a direct encounter with the Lord in which one person's mourning is turned into consolation. A widow, already without a husband, has just lost her only son when Jesus passes by his funeral procession in Nain (see Lk 7:11–17). She is in deep mourning, for she has now lost both her husband and son. The widow is completely vulnerable and alone in the world. The Lord Jesus acknowledges the tenderness of her mourning and has compassion on the widow. In seeing her profound grief and frailty, Jesus blesses and comforts her. He then orders the young man, dead to this world, to arise. He does as he is commanded; he sits up and greets his mother with happiness and open arms.

The widow of Nain was consoled by the power of God. Such a resuscitation of the dead is a rare occurrence in the Lord's public ministry, and yet he grants this most unique of all signs to this mournful person of Nain. This manifestation of his authority shows what God can do through those who are willing to endure the sufferings divine providence bestows on them. In the widow, the Lord saw purity, humility, and a sorrowful love that compelled him to draw near to her and grant her his consolation and peace.

In our own lives, we may not be privy to such a dramatic episode and blessing, but we know this is the solace and happiness that God wishes to grant to all of us, if only we choose to genuinely grieve over our sins, mourn the tragedies of the world, and seek his help. Archbishop Fulton Sheen wrote in his masterpiece *Life of Christ* that "the Cross must come before the crown. . . . There must be fellowship with His sufferings before there can be fellowship with His glory." If we seek the comfort that comes with sharing in his glory, we must join in the suffering of his cross.

Mourning in Gethsemane

The darker aspects of our culture form a callousness on our souls and breed an indifference to the sufferings of others. We can grow bitter with envy toward our neighbor, seeing them as mere obstacles or competitors to our own pleasures and ambitions. This cultural shift seeks to perpetuate a misery that falsely advertises itself as the solution to humanity's ills.

In such a scenario, it is a noticeable sign of contradiction for us to mourn humanity's sin and grieve over the wretchedness of the world. Such a summons to mourn is grounded in our awareness of truth, beauty, and goodness. Our sincere mourning over evil dispels the apathy we might otherwise feel toward the people and things around us because we don't see them as our competitors but rather sincerely wish for them to turn away from darkness. Our souls will remain open to God's providence and we will labor for the well-being of our neighbor. To the degree that we mourn, it can lead us to true consolation and happiness.

We see in the life of Jesus Christ a shining exemplar of what it means to take up the mantle of solemn mourning for the sins and sorrows of humanity. While the Lord Jesus fulfilled this call throughout his life, it was concentrated and fulfilled in the paschal mystery; namely, his passion, death, and resurrection.

In the garden of Gethsemane, the place where the harvest of the Mount of Olives was pressed (olives becoming oil), the Lord Jesus accepted an avalanche of mourning as he allowed his own body and soul to be crushed in order that God could make all things new (cf. Rv 21:5). As the Lord fell to the ground and his sweat turned to blood, and with a heart wrenched by grief, he cried out, "My Father, if it be possible, let this cup pass from me" (Mt 26:39).

With his apostles succumbing to their slumber, Jesus became sin itself (cf. 2 Cor 5:21). In doing so, he felt alone, isolated from humanity and rejected by God. In this abandonment, the Lord offered his mourning as the beginning of his saving work. Knowing of the Father's love and intimacy, Jesus accepted this alienation caused by sin. In the restlessness of his mourning and sorrowful heart, he surrendered without condition, saying to the Father, "Your will be done" (Mt 26:42).

As with Jesus, the Suffering Servant and Lamb of God, so with each of us. In our desire and search for happiness, we are called to walk with the Lord Jesus and be ready to mourn for the sins and sufferings of humanity.

Two Invitations

The life of the apostles and of the early Church are full of examples of mourning over darkness and tragedy. Of all such situations, one account stands out because it is the most binary and acute parallel of an invitation accepted and of an invitation refused. The Scriptures tell us the stories of Peter and Judas who, in their own way, each severely betrayed the Lord Jesus: Judas sold him out for thirty pieces of silver and Peter denied knowing him three times, even to the Lord's face.

Each of these men knew Jesus and his loving kindness, and they saw his miracles and heard his message of mercy. Both had the same opportunity to mourn their sins, repent, and receive the consolation of God. Each knew the authentic path back to happiness.

The Scriptures tell us that Judas refused the invitation to repent. Instead, he allowed shame to consume him and despair to poison his heart. He fell into the greatest of miseries and hanged himself from a tree (see Mt 27:3–5).

The Scriptures, however, also show us the opposite reaction in the story of St. Peter: "And the Lord turned and looked at Peter. And Peter remembered the word of the Lord, how he said to him, 'Before the cock crows today, you will deny me three times.' And he went out and wept bitterly" (Lk 22:61–62).

We see that Peter accepted the call to mourn his sins. In weeping bitterly, the chief apostle chose the path that vanquished his misery and allowed his grief to lead him back to the Lord and his consolation. Later, after Our Lord's resurrection, Peter is given mercy and a chance to reconcile his denial. Jesus asks him three times, "Do you love me?" and three times Peter confirms his love for Christ (see Jn 21:15–19), undoing the pain he caused with his three denials.

Note the distinction between despair and repentance here. It might seem that Judas mourned his sins since he was upset and ultimately hung himself. But regretting your actions and falling into despair is not the same as mourning; when we do this, we are not trusting in God's mercy, which offends him greatly; he said so to St. Faustina, which she recorded in her diary, *Divine Mercy in my Soul* (*Diary*, 628, 1486). The way Judas handled the aftermath of his betrayal might be compared to the person who despairs at the bedside of a dying relative and curses God rather than mourning the tragedy but trusting in his will. Peter would be the one who also cries beside the deathbed of his loved one but trusts that everything is a part of God's greater plan.

In summary, our first step should always be to realize what we have done is wrong, but where we go from there determines our path back to happiness. Will we despair like Judas or trust in God's mercy like Peter?

Mount to Mission

There are countless causes and endless reasons for us to mourn, from the loss of a loved one, to bad health, to broken relationships, to financial difficulties, to moral failings, to a whole host of other personal and social sins and tragedies. In these different situations, our mourning can help us along our path to happiness in many unexpected ways.

One such way is the capacity of our mourning to help us pray. As we grieve, we accept that we are powerless. This awareness can help us cry out to God in prayer, whether for a personal need of forgiveness, an appeal on behalf of someone else in serious sin, or a contrite spirit over the fallenness of our world and its evils. In turning to prayer, we are expressing our need and our confidence—at whatever level it might be—in God and his ability to absolve, heal, and restore what is bruised, broken, and lost.

As we pray, we find the virtue of hope growing within our souls. It's an accurate observation that the first fruit of prayer is hope. But hope is not confidence in ourselves; it is a greater reliance on God and his divine providence. Hope allows us to pray with authenticity, "Your will be done." Hope gives us the humility to recognize that we only see a small portion of reality and nurtures trust within us that, in the light of eternity, God's will is good and—however unknown or mysterious it might be—beneficial to everyone and to the common good of humanity. It is hope that echoes the biblical petition of a sick boy's father: "I believe; help my unbelief!" (Mk 9:24).

A story from my life some years ago conveys this message that mourning nurtures hope. I was called to the ICU for a man who was in a very bad accident. The family was there, and in my pastoral visit, after administering the Anointing of the Sick, we all prayed together. After we prayed, I assured the man's wife and children, "Everything will be all right."

As I left the room, one of the ICU nurses (who was a sporadic parishioner I knew) called me over and said, "Father, you have to be careful what you say. That patient is not doing well. I don't know if you should tell the family he's going to get better."

I was confused by the exchange. I said to her, "I didn't say the man was going to get better. I just reminded them that everything was going to be all right."

She gave a half-hearted smile and walked away. As I entered the elevator, I thought about the conversation. I realized that as believers refined by a mourning of the soul that opens us up to eternity, we know that regardless of our health, the medical sciences, emotional fragility, or the imminence of our own death, everything is going to be all right. This is hope given by a reliance on God.

Additionally, mourning is not just about loss but about the gratitude it develops within our souls. The cultural maxim is true that we don't appreciate what we have until it's gone or, by extension, until we know that it can be lost or taken away. As a priest, all too many times I hear people at the end of life wishing they had shared more time and expressed more of their love and affection to family and friends. Left to its own devices, our fallen nature can take time, opportunity, family, close friends, and even our relationship with God for granted. The loss of these gifts, or the awareness that they can be lost, helps us to grow in our thanksgiving to God and his many blessings. This gratitude is a tremendous help for us in our decision to be happy and to seek the consolation of God.

Likewise, in the struggles and sorrows of life, a spirit of mourning can breed compassion within us. When we mourn, we are better able to mourn with others, to understand and share empathy with our neighbors in their sufferings. This true compassion, unlike condescension, is a real *suffering with* the other person since it shows an equality in our shared hurt and vulnerability. Through compassion, we can suffer and mourn with one another and be an instrument of God's consolation to each other.

This compassion spills over and inspires fortitude. In contemporary societies, it's commonplace to see Christians attacked or mocked, especially by those claiming tolerance and acceptance. The social pressure to remain silent is so strong that the act of standing up and challenging this assault requires deep courage and conviction. Frequently, opposition to such a majority is met with persecution. This persecution can be physical or violent, financial or legal, but can also be expressed in social exclusion and character assassination. Words like bigot, racist, and bully are redefined and leveled as insults and degrading titles to those who hold true to Christian principles. In such a dilemma, those seeking righteousness are, perhaps in a surprising way, strengthened by their mourning of the evil plaguing our world. They mourn because they know they are aligned with Truth and their lost brothers and sisters are not, but in this realization, they are emboldened, knowing they stand with Christ Jesus, who was also persecuted for being a sign of contradiction in the world.

As we acknowledge the spiritual benefits of mourning over sin and sorrow, it might be helpful to look at a few general situations when they have been displayed in the trenches of life:

- The woman who loses her husband of fifty years and is in deep mourning. The grief runs the risk of covering her in darkness, but through her faith and hope, she chooses happiness and allows her suffering to become redemptive.

- The group of teenagers who make fun of a classmate and the person is visibly hurt by the insults. One of the group members grieves the sin, repents, and reaches out to the classmate in friendship and is rewarded with a sense of peace for doing the right thing.

- The parents who discover that their son has been viewing pornography on the family computer and grieve the sin of their child and its consequences on his soul. They approach him, wanting to free him from the sin, and are comforted by a difficult but therapeutic intervention that ends with a vow to move forward with purity.

- The married man who finds himself enjoying the flirtations of a female coworker and realizes that he is creating more opportunities to be around her, repents of the emotional adultery, and charitably avoids the other person, refocusing his affection back to his wife. In doing so, he lives with a newfound freedom of innocence that brings serenity to his everyday life.

- The politician who respectfully speaks the truth about the nature of marriage and is publicly mocked as a bigot and ostracized by his fellow citizens, and yet holds fast to the truth, offering up his suffering for the conversion of all people and sleeping easy at night knowing he is fighting for God's truth.

These are practical examples in everyday life. Each of us has our own list of how we can renew our decision for happiness in the way we grieve over evil and the fallenness of our world today.

Evil abounds, but grace abounds more (cf. Rom 5:20). Will we accept the humbling path of mourning and sorrow and allow it to refine our desire and search for happiness? The choice is ours.

Examination of Conscience

- Do I trust in God's care?

- Do I see mourning and sorrow as a path to salvation and happiness?

- Do I needlessly avoid grief and deny my sorrow?

- Am I willing to acknowledge my own pain and suffering and ask God for help?

- Do I feel contrition over my sins and regularly go to the sacrament of Reconciliation?

- Do I grieve over the sins or sufferings of loved ones and offer assistance to them in changing their lives or carrying their burdens?

- Do I give in to desolation or despair over the evil of our world or do I turn to God in prayer and ask for his blessing?

- Am I diligent in nurturing hope in my own soul and in those around me?

- Do I show compassion to others in their sufferings?

- Do I speak the truth with love and willingly accept any persecution for the sake of goodness?

School of Discipleship

Continuing in our School of Discipleship, it is now time to look at the second beatitude: **those who mourn.**

When we accept the mourning that comes to us, and when we mourn our own sins and those of the world, the Holy Spirit bestows the gift of **knowledge** upon us. This does not necessarily refer to what we think most often of knowledge, as in that obtained through education and reason. Rather, this is the knowledge of recognizing good and evil for what they are. We are given the knowledge of how much virtue pleases God and how much sin offends him.

Once we receive this gift, the virtue of **hope** is perfected in our soul, for if we have the knowledge of good and evil, we can hope to live a virtuous life and find salvation in Christ Jesus. The *Catechism* says of hope: "It keeps man from discouragement; it sustains him during times of abandonment; it opens up his heart in expectation of eternal beatitude" (CCC 1818). With hope, we are able to persevere in mourning, whether that is hoping for God's assistance and blessing during times of trial or hoping for his mercy after we have sinned. It is in our hope that we receive the promise of this beatitude, which is to be comforted. Hope fills us with certitude and consolation that goodness will triumph.

This beatitude, gift, and virtue help us to better understand the petition in the Lord's Prayer **"Thy will be done on earth as it is in heaven"** since knowledge and hope give us eyes to see eternity and the goodness in our world. They inspire us to pursue lives according to God's will. The blossoming of this petition leads us to the promise of this beatitude, for when we accept his will (even in times of mourning), we are comforted in ways beyond our understanding.

Lastly, the path that begins from this beatitude and crosses through these other aspects of the spiritual life helps us overcome the capital sin of **envy**. This sin craves for itself what properly belongs to God, or what graciously belongs to one's neighbor. It deflates hope and builds a kingdom of misery in the soul of the one who is enslaved to it. Just as we are blessed if we accept mourning (the loss of a good), the envious are unhappy in the good they see in someone else. If we mourn, we can share in another's sadness, but if we are envious, we are happy over another's failures and sad at another's success.

If we don't grieve over evil and surrender ourselves to God, then we will abandon hope, rationalize or succumb to darkness, lose gratitude, and perpetually crave what we do not have.

As the promise of those who mourn is consolation, so the punishment of the anti-beatitude is a restless spirit always bitter about the good that others have. The envious have an awkward discomfort with both themselves and the world around them.

In conclusion, the second row of our spiritual matrix looks like this:

BEATITUDE	GIFT OF THE SPIRIT	CORRESPONDING VIRTUE	PETITION OF THE LORD'S PRAYER	CAPITAL SIN/ ANTI-BEATITUDE
Blessed are those who mourn, for they shall be comforted	Knowledge	Hope	Thy will be done on earth as it is in heaven	Envy

Prayer

Gracious Father,

I want to be happy. Keep me from envy and the misery of this world.

Help me to hope in you and to always be docile to your will in my life.

I see the fallenness in my heart and in the world around me.

I'm in mourning and grief. I wait for you.

Come to me and bless me with your consolation.

Bring me into your kingdom! Bless me with happiness.

Through Christ our Lord. Amen.

Three Helpful Truths to Redemptive Mourning:

+ God's divine care of creation blesses me and covers all things.
+ No sin or evil can define or overwhelm me.
+ I am called to surrender everything to God, even the most painful or confusing things.

Wisdom of the Lord Jesus

Truly, truly, I say to you, you will weep and lament, but the world will rejoice; you will be sorrowful, but your sorrow will turn into joy. When a woman is in labor, she has pain, because her hour has come; but when she is delivered of the child, she no longer remembers the anguish, for joy that a child is born into the world. So you have sorrow now, but I will see you again and your hearts will rejoice, and no one will take your joy from you.

John 16:20–22

God's Humbling of Job

Then the Lord answered Job out of the whirlwind:

"Who is this that darkens counsel by words without knowledge?

Gird up your loins like a man, I will question you, and you shall declare to me.

Where were you when I laid the foundation of the earth? Tell me, if you have understanding.

Who determined its measurements—surely you know! Or who stretched the line upon it?

On what were its bases sunk, or who laid its cornerstone,

when the morning stars sang together, and all the sons of God shouted for joy?"

Job 38:1–7

— CHAPTER 3 —

THE MEEK

*Blessed are the meek, for they shall
inherit the earth.*

MATTHEW 5:5

The Meekness of a Galilean Fisherman

While a seminarian at the Pontifical North American College in Rome, one of my responsibilities was to give tours of the holy places to English-speaking pilgrims and tourists. Of the many sites to which I would take people, none of them compared to St. Peter's Basilica. This massive structure—the largest Christian church in the world—stands as a testament to faith in general and to the specific witness of the apostle buried beneath its main altar.

Simon Peter was an "uneducated, common" fisherman from Galilee (cf. Lk 5:1–11; Acts 4:13). He first met the Lord Jesus through his younger brother Andrew, who had been a disciple of St. John the Baptist and seemed to have been more religiously zealous than his older brother. Perhaps like many people in today's world, Simon was preoccupied with work and other concerns of life (cf. Acts 10:26). Jesus, however, broke through those distractions and called Simon to follow him, giving him the new name, Peter (see Jn 1:42).

Peter's meekness and sincerity endeared him to the Lord Jesus. He was a man who knew himself and who loved deeply. While at times he lacked what you might call diplomacy, Peter never attempted to mask his weaknesses, which are always apparent in the Sacred Scriptures. He wanted to be faithful and happy, recognizing his deep need for Jesus Christ and saying on one occasion, "Lord, to whom shall we go? You have the words of eternal life" (Jn 6:68). Unlike Judas Iscariot, when Simon Peter lacked fidelity—when he betrayed the person whom both God and he himself wanted to be—"he went out and wept bitterly" (Lk 22:62).

When the apostles are listed in the Gospels, Peter is the "first" (Mt 10:2). The designation is not given because of heightened virtue or achieved holiness but because of the authority bestowed upon him by the Lord Jesus (see Mt 16:18–19). This priority was given to him because of his humility, his confessed sinfulness, and the desire he had for God to save and restore him to grace. It's a clear expression of the Lord's teaching: "So the last will be first, and the first last" (Mt 20:16). Peter's position in the early Church, therefore, is more a reflection of God's generosity to those who seek him than to any perceived greatness or construed prominence of the man himself.

It is ultimately to Simon Peter, the meek fisherman and repentant traitor, that the Lord Jesus would say, "And I tell you, you are Peter, and on this rock I will build my Church, and the gates of Hades shall not prevail against it. I will give you the keys of the kingdom of heaven" (Mt 16:18–19). Jesus looked upon him with favor and blessed him with the inheritance of the earth as the first bishop of Rome.

How marvelous is the grand basilica—at 432,756 square feet, with a width of 461 feet and a length of 694 feet—as it bears witness to the impulsive but deferential apostle who had the boldness to answer the Lord's question, "Who do you say that I am?" with the declaration "You are the Christ, the Son of the living God" (Mt 16:15–16). The legacy of the simple Galilean fisherman outlives and outshines the mighty and powerful of the earth. His sanctuary continues to be a breathing basilica that gives millions of people hope and encouragement, while the columns and statues of the emperors and kings are mere museum pieces, lying in the dust of history.

This is the promise given to those who are willing to live a life of meekness and humility. It is to the lowly of the world that the inheritance of the earth is given. As we each look for happiness, we are called to be meek and to seek a life of reverence and openness to God. And to those who choose to avoid the dark passions of self-pity and wrath, which are born from a sense of displacement within the soul that seeks to control the world and deny who it is, God offers the peace of his kingdom. He gives the meek the entire world as their home and his own divine heart as a place of rest.

Defining Meekness

In the decisions we make throughout our lives, we either pursue the kingdom of happiness or some other kingdom; we cannot actively pursue both. If we choose to pursue happiness, then meekness is one of the necessary postures we must take up along the way.

Admittedly, meekness is one of the harder beatitudes to define. Is it just a reference to our social status or is it a disposition of our soul? Is meekness only a synonym for humility, patience, gentleness, respect, or kindness? The first answer is "yes," meekness is a disposition of our soul. Though being materially poor may help form meekness in our soul, it is not a requirement. Meanwhile, the answer to the second question is also "yes," as meekness absorbs and edifies other related virtues, those listed above and others.

But whether it is a disposition of our soul or a foundation for other virtues to stand on, meekness is not a singular act but a habit of virtue we must develop. To use a musical example, meekness is not a single cantor but the member of a choir who sometimes serves as the conductor so that the selected piece can be played well and beautifully. With this context in mind, what is a working definition of meekness?

Meekness is a level-headed, clear understanding and acceptance of who we are and where we stand in relation to God, our world, and our neighbor. It shows us ourselves spiritually the way a mirror shows us ourselves physically. But meekness doesn't just show us ourselves, it helps us to accept it. It is a strength of mind, heart, and body that gives us the inner resolve to claim and accept this self-identity. Meekness shows us our sin when we're in darkness, but also our dignity when we are feeling low or suffering humiliation. In either situation, meekness invites us to choose to live—in spite of internal or external adversity—a life of transparency and resignation.

Many times, meekness and strength are seen as opposing characteristics since the meek are usually mistreated by society. But paradoxically it is precisely meekness that gives us strength, though not strength as it is usually understood, such as in the one who has the most power, influence, or resources. Rather, meekness is a *gentle* strength within us. It gives us a poise that allows us to be at peace in our own skin while also empowering us to pour ourselves out in self-donation to others. As demonstrated by the Blessed Virgin Mary in her beautiful canticle to God:

> My soul magnifies the Lord,
> and my spirit rejoices in God my Savior,
> for he has regarded the low estate of his handmaiden.
> For behold, henceforth all generations will call me
> blessed;
> For he who is mighty has done great things for me,
> and holy is his name. (Lk 1:46–49)

Mary was in no position of power, and she admits this by referencing her "low estate." This is that element of self-realization in meekness, knowing your place before God. But she also knew "all generations would call her blessed," meaning she also knew of the great honor God was bestowing upon her, and she would carry that honor with a "gentle strength" that we know all too well as her spiritual children.

We know the Virgin Mary had no sin within her, but in our own lives, meekness provides the strength we need to overcome jealousy, wrath, envy, and the fluidity of our passions. It is the internal power that fortifies us to remain consistent with truth and goodness in the face of challenges and distress. In times of recklessness, when our actions are rash or foolish, meekness brings us back in order.

Additionally, the meek, in knowing their own sinfulness and the dangers of pride and wrath, are slow to violence and labor to settle affairs with gentle hands and tender hearts. They seek to understand their neighbors and are inclined to empathy and compassion.

Our willingness to be meek is an affirmation of our desire for happiness. How can anyone be happy if they're not willing to acknowledge and accept who they are and where they stand before God and their neighbor? No one living a lie or playing some demented game of denial can be happy. A person living in such darkness is stuck in their make-believe world, and the fullness of the earth promised by God to those who are meek will never be theirs.

Meekness in the Temple

Jesus's life is a paradigm of meekness. But when we look at the Gospels, some might be rattled by the event of his purification of the Temple. What was Jesus doing when he seemingly lost his temper here? Let's look at this scene so that we can better understand it.

It was almost time for the Jewish Passover, and Jesus had gone to the temple courts in Jerusalem. In the courts, merchants were selling cattle, sheep, and doves while others were sitting at tables exchanging money.

Seeing that his Father's house had been turned into a "den of robbers," Jesus made a whip out of cords and drove them out of the temple courts. He scattered the coins of the money changers and overturned their tables (see Mt 21:12–13). The Lord's disciples were shaken by the scene, but then they remembered that it is written: "Zeal for your house will consume me" (cf. Ps 69:9; Jn 2:17).

As with the initial response of the disciples, so many people might be shocked by the Lord's actions in the Temple. Is this a blaring exception to a life otherwise marked by meekness?

In fact, there is no exception. The Lord was as meek in this situation with the merchants as he was to the repentant woman (see Lk 7:36–48) or to the sick and suffering who sought healings (cf. Mt 8:14–16), or to the children who sought his blessing (see Mt 19:13–15). But how is this possible? Isn't meekness an expression of gentleness and compassion?

Yes, as we noted before, meekness can edify these virtues. But meekness can also inspire other virtues such as justice, righteous anger, obedience, and temperance. Meekness isn't about "warm fuzzies," about making ourselves and others feel good, or about being a push-over or a weakling. Meekness helps us pursue happiness by faithfully fulfilling our vocation and the duties of our state in life, and by always seeking God's glory and the common good of our neighbors.

For example, it's meek for loving parents to discipline their children when they have misbehaved, even though the children are made uncomfortable and the punishment is unpleasant to them (and the parents). At times, parents may have to exercise justice over gentleness, temperance of affection over tenderness, or righteous anger over patience. In many different scenarios, the meekness of parents—always tempered by reason and goodness—is rightly expressed in a severe way so that their children will comprehend the darkness of the bad actions and grasp the importance of the virtuous ones.

Now, let us return to Jesus's cleansing of the Temple. As the anointed Savior, the Lord lived for the glory of God the Father and the redemption of humanity. In light of his vocation and the saving work entrusted to him, he was completely within the realm of meekness to exercise justice and discipline to those who were degrading the Temple.

With this awareness, we can place this episode in the Temple alongside the Lord's tenderness with the woman at Jacob's well (see Jn 4:4–26) as consistent examples of his meekness. In summary, therefore, meekness is not necessarily passive, but always proper to the vocation given to us. It is a means to self-awareness and acceptance, and a sure path to happiness and the inheritance of the earth. It's an invitation to be ourselves and to labor for virtue and holiness. If we choose this life of humility, then the Lord can come to us and exalt us, and ultimately bless us with happiness.

Meekness in the Apostolic Ministry

This meekness of the Lord inspired and enlivened the early Church and continues to feed the spiritual treasury of the faithful throughout the ages. In the first generation of the faith, the apostles knew the sacred responsibilities given to them. In showing their meekness through boldness, they spread the Gospel from Spain to India and from Macedonia to North Africa.

For his part, St. Peter arrived in Rome about AD 42 (cf. 1 Pt 5:13). After preaching and teaching for many years, including to St. Mark, who sat at Peter's feet when he penned his own Gospel, our first pope became the target of Emperor Nero's fury against the Christians. In AD 67, the emperor searched for Peter, prompting the Galilean to flee the city in fear. But as he left, he saw an image of the Risen Lord. Peter asked him, "Lord, where are you going?" Jesus replied that he was going back to Rome to be crucified again. Peter was humbled and found the strength to return to the city. He was captured and carried to Nero's circus, where he "did not wish to go" (Jn 21:18); yet, "Greater love has no man than this, that a man lay down his life for his friends" (Jn 15:13).

Upon returning, the emperor declared that this first bishop of Rome would be crucified like his Christ. In an unusual request, St. Peter, showing his humility, petitioned to be crucified upside down because he did not consider himself worthy to be crucified in the same manner as his Lord. Nero granted the request and the first pope sanctified Rome with his papal blood. St. Peter, imitating the meekness of his Lord, accepted his vocation and the duties given to him by God.

We see in the life of St. Peter a model and encouragement for us to live meekly in our own circumstances and to discern our responsibilities and perform them with virtue and goodness.

Showing Meekness in the Face of Mockery

Jesus exemplifies meekness to us in many ways, through patience, charity, and forgiveness, but above all, he is the model of meekness through acceptance. Jesus accepted his unjust condemnation, his sufferings, and his passion and death. The Lord did not beg for his life, he did not fight against the guards, he did not avoid anguish or try to run away, but instead, he accepted his saving mission, as torturous and humiliating as it was for him. And in his agony and pain, he prayed not for vengeance but for mercy toward his offenders: "Father, forgive them; for they know not what they do" (Lk 23:34).

The Lord Jesus's sacrifice was a direct example of meekness.

Arrested, sentenced, and abused, he nursed no wrath, fueled no pride, and offered no counter-violence.

In the Lord, we find only love and mercy. Though his example is a very severe one, it provides a lesson for us in less-than-severe instances when we need to be meek. It teaches us that if our God can give his life in meekness and humility, then we can forgive our neighbor, avoid wrath, and show respect to others, even those who mock or mistreat us.

Mount to Mission

There are many ways to incorporate meekness into our daily lives. This is due in part to the fact that meekness involves our vocation and the full array of the duties of our state in life. Meekness collaborates with other virtues, such as patience, gentleness, kindness, justice, temperance, and many more, in order to help us live a good and holy life.

In particular, meekness runs hand-and-hand with humility. We cannot have meekness without humility. As Jesus is the supreme example of meekness, so he is also the highest example of humility. The Lord lived humbly all the way from his birth in a forgotten stable to his death on the cross. In our lives, how can we show greater meekness and humility?

In seeking to be meek, the ordering of our emotions is central to this way of life. On any given day, our emotions are pushed and tried. People's idiosyncrasies (or even our own) can drive us to anger, sadness, and self-pity. From little things, such as being late to work or a customer being rude to us at our job, to greater things, such as poor health, financial difficulties, or marital problems, so much can give us cause for intense anger toward others or ourselves. In each area of our lives, our reactions must be meek. We must be true to ourselves in accord with God's divine plan. We must have a strong self-awareness of our own sinfulness and observe a tempered justice in our judgments of others. With true meekness, we must forgive the small and large assaults on our lives and keep them from ruling over us. We are called to be generous and universal with our mercy.

It might be helpful for us to evaluate a few general situations in the trenches of life that are aided by meekness:

- A driver on a daily commute to work who is cut off in traffic and rather than react with wrath—"road rage"—instead keeps a cool head and continues to drive with temperance and charity.

- An army drill sergeant who is loud and demanding in order to prepare a new soldier for military proficiency and responsibilities but is also tempered by reason and justice, knowing that such an approach is for a specific purpose and not acceptable civil behavior in society.

- The teacher who humbly realizes that some students are not grasping the course content as quickly as others and so graciously makes time for extra tutoring and guidance, ensuring every student can learn and have mutual opportunities.

- The parents who know their son is lying to them and, rather than fuel rage, attempt to show the child the darkness caused by his lies and gently guide him to an acknowledgment of his fault and a request for forgiveness.

- The talented musician who, when her ability is recognized, feels embarrassed by the attention but realizes she can use her talent to glorify God and so joins her church choir.

These are practical examples in our everyday lives. Each of us has our own list of how we can choose happiness through meekness. And so, will we accept the path of humility and allow it to reshape and mold us for the kingdom of happiness? The choice is ours.

Examination of Conscience

- Do I seek to know myself, both the good and the bad?
- Do I find myself envious or jealous of the accomplishments or possessions of others?
- Am I quick to forgive a person who has hurt or offended me or a loved one?
- Am I able to order my emotions according to reason and goodness?
- Am I open to humbly accepting criticism or discipline?
- Do I seek to give others the credit they are due?
- Do I offer tempered corrections to problems without adding insult?
- Am I prone to wrath or violence toward others in confusing or tense moments?
- Do I reverence God in my life and regularly attend Sunday Mass?
- Do I accept suffering as a part of life that will strengthen my bond with God?

School of Discipleship

Continuing in our School of Discipleship, it is now time to look at the third beatitude: **the meek.**

If we are meek, the Holy Spirit will bestow us with the gift of **piety**. This gift of the Holy Spirit guides us in reverence toward God and his providential care. It might best be described as affection for God, which is instilled in us from our conception, but can be nurtured throughout life. If we have this affection for God, we will "inherit the earth," for he will return that affection and make us his sons and daughters, and as his children, we share in the inheritance of what is his, which includes the earth (see Ps 24:1). Through piety, we remain a part of his kingdom on earth, the Church.

Once we receive this gift, the virtue of **justice** is perfected in our soul, which gives to others their proper due. As we honor God in piety, we are led to respect our neighbor through justice. The *Catechism* says that justice "is the moral virtue that consists in the constant and firm will to give their due to God and neighbor.... The just man, often mentioned in Sacred Scriptures, is distinguished by the habitual right thinking and the uprightness of his conduct toward his neighbor" (CCC 1807). Since the meek have an accurate view of their place before God and in relation to their neighbor, it is easy to see how justice would be perfected through this beatitude.

This beatitude, gift, and virtue help us better understand the petition in the Lord's Prayer **"Thy Kingdom Come"** in that we inherit the world and already share in some portion of God's kingdom here on earth (the Church). The meek person has true piety toward God and prays sincerely, "Thy kingdom come."

Lastly, the path that begins from this beatitude and crosses through these other aspects of the spiritual life helps us overcome the capital sin of **wrath**, or anger. This sin is the opposite of meekness, piety, and justice. The person stuck in wrath is less worried about God's kingdom and more worried about his own.

Wrath is the use of force—emotional, physical, or by some other means—to assume power and to control life. As meekness wins us the inheritance of the earth, wrath shrinks the world into the very small sphere of our own dominance and manipulation.

Meek people order their emotions toward virtue, seeking both knowledge of themselves and justice for their neighbors. They understand that wrath must be tempered by reason so that it becomes righteous anger. They have a spiritual openness that allows God to give the whole earth to them as a home and a place of peace. People consumed with wrath, however, are slaves to their passions and inclinations.

Wrath robs the person of their rationality and of their personality. It takes over all other emotions and becomes a tyrant within the person's very soul. The world becomes very small, stifling, and dizzy. As meekness helps us remain calm so we can fulfill our duties, wrath's unchecked energy carries us past what we are called to do so that we infringe upon others' dignity, as well as our own, thus forfeiting justice.

As the promise of meekness is inheriting the earth, so the punishment of the anti-beatitude is a small world unsettled by angry passions where we attempt to usurp control away from God.

In conclusion, the third row of our spiritual matrix looks like this:

BEATITUDE	GIFT OF THE SPIRIT	CORRESPONDING VIRTUE	PETITION OF THE LORD'S PRAYER	CAPITAL SIN/ ANTI-BEATITUDE
Blessed are the meek, for they shall inherit the earth	Piety	Justice	Thy kingdom come	Wrath

Prayer

Loving Father,

I want to be happy. Help me to be meek and humble of heart.

Your kingdom come!

Grant me peace and keep wrath far from me as I deal with myself and others.

Teach me your ways. Show me your love and mercy.

I wait for you.

Come to me, Father, and bless me with your inheritance.

Bring me into your kingdom! Show me happiness.

Through Christ our Lord. Amen.

Three Helpful Truths to Be Meek of Heart:

+ I am who I am, with my strengths and weaknesses before me.

+ God will shape and mold me into the person I should be.

+ My way to happiness and holiness is virtue, in service to meekness, according to my state in life.

Example of the Lord Jesus

When Herod saw Jesus, he was very glad, for he had long desired to see him, because he had heard about him, and he was hoping to see some sign done by him. So he questioned him at some length; but he made no answer. The chief priests and the scribes stood by, vehemently accusing him. And Herod with his soldiers treated him with contempt and mocked him; then, clothing him in gorgeous apparel, he sent him back to Pilate.

Luke 23:8–11

The Psalmist's Wonder

When I look at your heavens,
the work of your fingers,
the moon and the stars which you have established;
what is man that you are mindful of him,
and the son of man that you care for him?

Psalm 8:3–4

CHAPTER 4

Those Who Hunger and Thirst for Righteousness

Blessed are those who hunger and thirst for righteousness, for they shall be satisfied.

MATTHEW 5:6

A True Hunger, A Deep Thirst

Early in my priestly ministry, I frequently visited homebound and hospitalized Catholics. Some were practicing the Faith, others were hit-and-miss, and a few others were fallen away but open to the idea of periodically seeing a priest. As I made my visits, I came to know many of these folks and the stories of their lives. One gentleman, in particular, stands out in my memory; I'll call him Richard. He appeared to be a kind soul, frequently reading his Bible and saying his prayers and always acting graciously toward me.

As time moved along, Richard began to lose his eyesight from age and diabetes. It was a hard blow for him but one he came to accept and offer up for his loved ones.

In speaking about his loved ones, he shared with me the

tragic story of his life. The man I came to know was not the man that his former spouse, children, and extended family knew. He was not the man known to his employers or neighbors throughout the years. Richard described himself as a "wicked son of a gun." Most of his life was a twisted tale of alcohol and drug abuse, domestic violence, infidelity, embezzlement, identity theft, child abuse, swindling, squatting, and a host of other sins and crimes against both God and his neighbor. In listening to the narrative of his life, I felt shock, confusion, and distress, but mostly compassion for both him and his family.

What most moved me to compassion toward Richard was the witness of his sincere repentance and genuine desire for reconciliation with God and those whom he hurt. In describing the dark stories of his life, his voice often cracked and he was moved to tears; he would blush, look away, and observe deferential moments of prayer. On top of these observable traits, he was also very connected to the Bible and the hope it gave him. It was this love for the written Word of God that caused him such serious spiritual suffering when he began to lose his eyesight.

In my last few times with him, Richard would ask me to read accounts in the Bible that showed the mercy of God and his gentleness toward the sinner. As he listened to the stories, I could see the great consolation and peace they gave to his soul. When Richard passed away, no one requested his body or any type of memorial service. In working with people in the community, I offered a private service for him. After the service, his landlord gave me his well-read, beat-up, old Bible. It was a poignant gift since I understood how important it had been to him.

As I looked through it, I found what appeared to be a typical bookmark. But on the back was written—in shaky, hard-to-read penmanship—the simple yet radically profound half-written verse "Blessed are they who hunger and thirst." It was clear that Richard was not even able to finish writing the verse. It may have been the last thing he wrote before he went blind.

Either way, the half-written verse best summarized the deep hope and heartfelt longing of this repentant sinner as his life came to an end. In spite of the horrible sins of his life, Richard turned to the Lord Jesus. He truly hungered and thirsted for holiness. And as the Lord promised, this man received his fill.

The story of this one person's life can be an inspiration to each of us as we pursue a life of happiness and holiness. Regardless of our past, with whatever sins of commission and omission we might have on our soul, the Lord will answer our call and provide fulfillment to anyone who truly seeks him.

Hardwired for Happiness

In life, we can hunger and thirst for many things. Most practically, for food and water. But we can also hunger and thirst for love and acceptance, wealth or status, health or power. Hunger can be diverse and multifaceted, from what is necessary to sustain life (food, water, etc.) to what is preferred for an easy life (like money). As we consider and ponder our thirst and hunger, we shouldn't forget to pay attention to our souls. The Lord Jesus promises satisfaction to all those who hunger and thirst for holiness. So what do we hunger and thirst for?

As human beings, we hold a unique dignity and have a

sacred role in the world. The story of creation tells us, "So God created man in His own image, in the image of God he created him; male and female he created them" (Gn 1:27).

Being made in God's very image bestows both privileges and responsibilities upon each person and upon the entire human family.

God began a process of revelation after creating us in his image, unveiling truths about himself and calling us to greater communion (a communion our first parents had but forfeited). In the fullness of time, God the Father sent his Son, the Lord Jesus Christ, to show us the face of God (cf. Gal 4:4–5). In this disclosure—this intimate sharing—the Most High shows us that in his innermost being he is not solitude, but family. God reveals himself as the Divine Family of the Father, Son, and Holy Spirit. It is in the image of this Divine Family that each of us was created, and it is from this Divine Family that each of us is loved (cf. Jn 3:16; Eph 1:3–12). As St. John beautifully explains it, "Beloved, let us love one another; for love is of God, and he who loves is born of God and knows God. He who does not love does not know God; for God is love. In this the love of God was manifest among us, that God sent his only begotten Son into the world, so that we might live through Him. In this is love, not that we loved God but that he loved us and sent his Son to be the expiation for our sins" (1 Jn 4:7–10).

So that we can appreciate the gift of life that we have received, it might be helpful to spell some things out. For example, we should understand that God is infinitely perfect. He does not need to be changed, adjusted, or upgraded. He does not have any weakness or imperfection. No one can add to the glory that he already possesses within himself. God is

doing just fine. As elementary as it might seem, we should
stress that God is all-perfect through the ages; this is why we
pray: "Glory be to the Father, and the Son, and the Holy
Spirit, as it was in the beginning, is now, and ever shall be,
world without end. Amen."

Within his perfection, God is infinitely blessed in himself.
He is Beatitude and Happiness itself. These truths are very
significant since it shows us that God wasn't serving some
divine need or looking for friends when he created us. God
did not make us because he was lonely. He didn't bring us
into existence because he has insecurity problems and needs
constant suppliants to remind him how wonderful and great
he is. God's life is one of beatitude, not misery or uncertainty.
God shares a consummate communion and blessing within
himself for all ages and it's a union that he offers to each of us.
In other words, he is completely satisfied.

Knowing of this revelation of God, we can now understand how much he loves us. God created us in sheer goodness
so as to generously share what he already held within himself. The Holy Trinity wants to impart and bestow the love
and happiness that is eternally exchanged between them. This
should fill us with tremendous joy and give direction to our
lives. On bad days, we can be encouraged by the reminder, "I
only exist because Someone loves me."

The above truths help us realize that we are made by and
for God. Since we are all made in such a fashion, we are hard-
wired for worship, happiness, and union with God. In our
lives and in our culture, we can find a litany of apparent goods
that claim to fill the *capax Dei*, which is our capacity for God,
oftentimes called the "God hole" within us. As much as we
might try in so many ways to fill this hole and pursue a false

happiness in other things, we are only led to the humbling acknowledgement that we and the world around us are finite and imperfect, and that neither we nor the things of creation (even those things that are inherently good) can completely fulfill us. We need to turn to God. Only in him will our hunger and thirst be satisfied.

This sentiment is echoed by the fourth-century bishop St. Augustine who famously wrote, "You have made us for yourself, O Lord, and our hearts are restless until they rest in you."

Who Tells Us Who We Are?

A story might help to stress this point. After my initial years as a priest, I was appointed to do vocations work. With my new duties, I wasn't able to exercise some of the usual responsibilities of a priest, such as visiting nursing homes. But since I frequently visited my parents, I made a habit of visiting a local assisted living facility. In time, some of the residents began to recognize me. This reminded me of a popular story of a priest who also visited nursing homes.

On one occasion, one of the residents was sitting in the hallway staring at him. At first he didn't pay her any attention, but eventually he couldn't ignore her gaze and so he walked over to say hello. The priest figured she must have identified him, but he asked, "Do you know who I am?" She just looked at him, prompting him to repeat the question, "Do you know who I am?" She continued to look right at him, sighed, and said, "No, . . . but if you ask the nurse, she'll tell you!"

While funny, the story emphasizes the point: If we want to be blessed, fulfilled, and happy, the answer will not come from ourselves, this fallen world, its pomp and vanities, or sin

and darkness. If we want to be fulfilled, we must look to God.
He made us—he's the "divine nurse" who can tell us who we
are—and our longing will only be fruitful when it's directed
to him and his kingdom. For any of us to be complete as
human beings—to be truly ourselves—we have to hunger
and thirst for a right ordering of our affections, desires, and
passions toward God and his will. We need to pine for his
righteousness in our lives.

Not by Bread Alone

As each of us has no doubt felt the pain of a false happiness
failing to deliver on its promises, so in a similar way, the Lord
Jesus was faced with the allure of false promises. After his baptism, Jesus was led by the Holy Spirit into the desert. It was
a time of preparation for his public ministry, and so he was
fasting for forty days and forty nights; not surprisingly, he was
hungry.

The evil one came to him and said, "If you are the Son of
God, command these stones to become loaves of bread." But
Jesus responded, "It is written, 'Man shall not live by bread
alone, but by every word that proceeds from the mouth of
God'" (Mt 4:3–5). This response shows us that our earthly
hunger and thirst point to a deeper spiritual hunger and thirst
for God.

After the first temptation, the devil continued with his
attack and took Jesus to the Temple in Jerusalem. He had him
stand on a pinnacle and said, "If you are the Son of God,
throw yourself down; for it is written: He will give his angels
charge of you, and on their hands they will bear you up, lest
you strike your foot against a stone" (Mt 4:5–6).

What an utter shock and depravity that the evil one would quote the Sacred Scriptures in order to manipulate the Lord into sin! And yet, Jesus boldly asserted, "Again it is written, 'You shall not tempt the Lord your God'" (Mt 4:7). We can only imagine the devil's dismay as Jesus directed his desires and longings to God the Father and not to entertainment and the spectacular. Jesus corrected the evil one's abuse of the Scriptures and sought his fulfillment from God alone.

A third time, the evil one took him to a very high mountain, showed him the nations of the world, and said to him, "All these I will give you, if you will fall down and worship me" (Mt 4:9). How appalling for the evil one to think that the Lord Jesus would abandon his Father for vanity and power. Not in these passing and incomplete things would Jesus place his hope and his hunger, but instead once again turn to God and thirst for his fellowship and righteousness. And so, Jesus commanded, "Begone, Satan! for it is written, 'You shall worship the Lord your God and him only shall you serve.'"

After these three temptations, all of which were a summary of the waywardness that lead us to misery, the devil left Jesus and angels came and cared for him.

In each of our lives, we have our own temptations that lie to us, distract us, and promise us what they cannot fulfill. Our hunger and thirst are misplaced in them, as convincing or attractive as they might be, since they cannot fill us up, but only leave is empty, desolate, and confused.

Lazarus and the Rich Man

In his Gospel account, St. Luke tells us the story of Lazarus, a poor man who starves to death while waiting for scraps of food from a rich man's table (see Lk 16:19–21). After his death, the poor man is given everlasting peace and contentment. The rich man, however, who devoted his life to wealth and riches (even to the neglect of a starving poor man) is given eternal punishment.

Those who are rich are not condemned because of their wealth, but because they allow their spiritual hunger and thirst to be eclipsed by material comfort. This is when wealth becomes a hindrance and a harm to a person's growth. It's when a scab is placed over the "God hole" in our souls and a false security is indulged that we have somehow fulfilled ourselves and all our needs. The rich man in the story fell into this trap. It's a delusion that creates a hell on earth. The rich man thought everything was fulfilled and so did not seek righteousness from God. If he had, he would have been led to notice—to give the most basic attention—to the poor man and his very human necessities of food and drink.

The rich and poor alike must remind themselves that, unlike physical hunger, spiritual hunger can only be satisfied by God.

St. Philip and the Eunuch

As we reflect on our spiritual hunger and thirst, we can turn to the Acts of the Apostles for encouragement. In particular, we can look at the superb example of the Ethiopian eunuch (see Acts 8:26–40). In this account, the eunuch is a powerful figure of the treasury. He is reading and struggling to understand the prophet Isaiah—hungering for spiritual wisdom—but he cannot find the answers by himself.

The apostle Philip, guided by the Holy Spirit, is sent to

the eunuch's chariot. The apostle asks, "Do you understand what you are reading?" The eunuch, showing great humility and a thirst for God, replied, "How can I, unless someone explains it to me?" (Acts 8:30–31) He invites Philip to come up and sit with him and teach him about Jesus Christ.

After St. Philip presents the Gospel to him, the eunuch sees water and asks Philip, "See, here is water. What is to prevent my being baptized?" (Acts 8:36–37). The apostle agreed and the eunuch ordered the chariots to be stopped. They both went down into the water and the eunuch was baptized. After the baptism, the Holy Spirit took Philip from the eunuch's sight.

In this encounter, a person's hunger and thirst were fulfilled. The eunuch, perhaps like many people on the peripheries today, was seeking spiritual wisdom and grace, and God sent him someone to satisfy that longing. If we allow ourselves to pine for God, he will not leave us unfulfilled. He will not treat us as orphans but will always be there to help us and perpetually welcome us into the fellowship of his Divine Family.

Mount to Mission

When we see the inability of this world to make us complete, we turn to the God who created us, loves us, and calls us into fellowship with him. We turn especially to the Eucharist—the Bread of Life—which is the Lord's presence among us. The Eucharist is the foretaste of our complete contentment in eternity with God.

It is significant that this, the Lord's enduring presence through time, comes to us through bread, which is a universal symbol of full bellies and good meals. In choosing bread,

the Lord shows us that his presence is the means to fulfillment; the Eucharist nourishes us while also leading us to an
everlasting contentment. Truly, therefore, the Eucharist is the
source and summit of our entire way of life as the children of
God. It is both a reflection of our eternal home and the food
we need to get there. Like an appetizer to the main course,
this "bread of angels" prepares us here to receive the full meal
at the Lord's banquet in heaven. We must strive to receive the
Eucharist as much as we are able, attending Mass each Sunday,
and daily when we are able.

Nourished by the Eucharist, therefore, we also pray. We
want to talk and listen to God in our everyday lives. We need
his counsel and wisdom. By extension, we read the Bible and
try to find the right worldview of a child of God. We allow
for the transformation of our minds through the written
Word of God so that we can know what is good and pleasing
and perfect to him (cf. Rom 12:1–2).

In particular, when we learn to rely on God, we will turn
to him in moments of anxiety, emptiness, and confusion. We
beg him to come to us, as St. Peter did as he sunk into the
waters, "Lord, save me!" (Mt 14:30). And we know that as
with Peter, so with us; he will stretch out his hand and lift us
up out of the tides in which we are drowning. This is a hunger
and thirst that is expressed in trust and dependency.

This spiritual awareness forms a life of virtue, especially
fortitude, patience, kindness, and perseverance. We come to
understand that virtues are good habits that allow God's grace
to work in and through us every day. We hunger and thirst for
this grace and for the presence of God.

This hunger then refines our sense of justice. We can
see, with new eyes, the sufferings and sorrows of our fellow

human beings, prompting us to serve and help them as much as we are able. This move toward justice flourishes in charity and generosity to our neighbors.

In our world today, there are many general examples of how others have lived out their hunger and thirst for righteousness. Here are a few:

- The man who works two jobs, is attentive to his family, and is a good neighbor. He has very little extra time, but knowing how much he needs the Lord, he makes a Holy Hour every week at his local parish.

- A man of great wealth who has the humility to realize how much his life has become about him. He examines his conscience and chooses to become involved in local outreaches to the poor.

- The young person who recognizes that she is in an unhealthy, dependent relationship with her boyfriend. She turns to God as her source of happiness and makes the difficult decision to put boundaries in her relationship with her boyfriend.

- The family who has not attended Mass all year but comes at Christmas and, seeing a spiritual void in their lives, comes to an awareness of their need for regular worship and so resolves to attend Mass every Sunday.

- The retired man who worked hard in life, is enjoying his retirement, and believes he has it all, and yet constantly feels that something is missing. After years of being away from the Church, he goes to confession and asks God for guidance.

- The college student studying under great scholars in many different fields and yet feels odd that all his studying doesn't involve anything about God, and so decides to include a regular reading of the Bible and the *Catechism of the Catholic Church* in his weekly schedule.

In all these ways and an array of others, we are all called to pursue happiness by a hunger and thirst for holiness. As we do so, we find an interior drive to pray and to exercise virtue, especially fortitude, as we seek God and his righteousness in our own lives and in our world today.

Examination of Conscience

- Do I realize that I was made by and for God?
- Do I regularly read the Bible or study Church teachings so as to better know God and my natural desire for him?
- Do I seek ways to nourish my soul, especially through the Eucharist and through prayer and other acts of piety?
- Do I generously give my time to others when they need help?
- Am I appreciative of my blessings in life (my home, family, work)?
- Do I pursue false sources of contentment and avoid spiritual hunger?
- Do I share my wealth with the less fortunate?
- Do I seek to be self-sufficient and ignore my natural thirst for God and spiritual things?
- Is my lifestyle one that indulges sloth?
- Do I respond to God's initiatives and share the Gospel with others?

School of Discipleship

Continuing in our School of Discipleship, it is now time to look at the fourth beatitude: **hungering and thirsting for righteousness.**

If we hunger and thirst for righteousness, or holiness, the Holy Spirit bestows us with the gift of **fortitude**, which the *Catechism* tells us "ensures firmness in difficulties and constancy in the moral life" (CCC 1808). Through fortitude, we conquer temptations and fears, even fear of death, as so many martyrs have shown. If this beatitude of hungering for holiness tells us we will be "satisfied," then it should not surprise us that we will be given fortitude; just as a well-fed and satisfied body will be strong when it faces threats, so will the well-fed soul be when temptation attacks. The holiness we seek and then consume is like valuable protein that strengthens us.

Once we receive this gift, the virtue of **courage** is perfected in our soul. Today, many use these two words (fortitude and courage) interchangeably. The difference for our purposes is that fortitude is a gift donated to us, which then enables us to be courageous. Fortitude is the input, while courage is the output if you will. We are only able to be courageous in the face of temptation and fear because we are enriched with fortitude. As we stay the course with fortitude, we are led to uphold virtue and honor our neighbor through courage.

This beatitude, gift, and virtue help us to better understand the petition in the Lord's Prayer **"Give us this day our daily bread."** Twice in this petition—"this day" and "daily"—do we stress our complete dependency on God and our awareness that we are fulfilled only in him. This fulfillment comes from the True Bread, the Eucharist. When we say we are hungering for holiness, we might as well say we are hungering for the Eucharist. The blossoming of this petition leads us to the promise of this beatitude, which is to be satisfied. Like a content belly after a good meal, the soul is satisfied and made holy by receiving the Eucharist.

Lastly, the path that begins from this beatitude and crosses through these other aspects of the spiritual life helps us unmask the deception of the capital sin of **sloth**. This anti-beatitude of hungering and thirsting is a spiritual indifference and a willful laziness, especially toward our soul and our natural desire for God. Physical laziness is an aspect of sloth, but this is not a complete definition. A man could work eighty hours a week and be materially driven to achieve success and still be slothful because he is "lazy" when it comes to tending for his soul. This person stuck in sloth is focused more on his own self-sufficiency and comfort than on the kingdom of God.

The satisfaction of spiritual hunger and thirst cannot be given to us when we are unwilling to put our spirit to work. For example, a person who lacks mercy cannot be forgiven. The person who is unkind cannot know kindness. The one who restricts love makes it difficult for them to be loved.

If we neglect our spiritual hunger and suppress our thirst for holiness, then sloth wins and self-indulgence sets in. Try as we might, with all that we can muster, we will not be content with ourselves, other people, or our world. We will be stuck in a cycle of nervousness, denial, agitation, momentary euphoria, melancholy, and rampant anxiety. In short, we will be perpetually hungry and thirsty and unable to be fulfilled.

As the promise of hungering and thirsting for righteousness is becoming satisfied, so the punishment of the anti-beatitude is a jaded, tired, and empty soul that lacks the nourishment it needs to fight evils and temptations.

In conclusion, the fourth row of our spiritual matrix looks like this:

BEATITUDE	GIFT OF THE SPIRIT	CORRESPONDING VIRTUE	PETITION OF THE LORD'S PRAYER	CAPITAL SIN/ ANTI-BEATITUDE
Blessed are those who hunger and thirst for righteous-ness, for they shall be satisfied	Fortitude	Courage	Give us this day our daily bread	Sloth

Prayer

Good and gracious God,
I want to be happy. And I wait on you.
Give me today all that I need. I trust in you.
Grant me your peace and keep sloth far from me.
Help me to rely on you. Teach me your ways.
Give me your strength and guidance.
Come to me, Father, and fulfill me
Bring me into your kingdom! Show me happiness.
Through Christ our Lord. Amen.

Three Helpful Truths to Remain Hungry and Thirsty for Righteousness:

+ I was made by and for God.

+ It's good to enjoy the things of this world but only God can give me complete contentment.

+ As I hunger and thirst, I'm called to see the hunger and thirst of others and help them as I'm able.

The Desire of the Lord Jesus

I glorified you on earth, having accomplished the work which you gave me to do; and now, Father, glorify me in your own presence with the glory which I had with you before the world was made.

John 17:4–5

The Psalmist's Wonder

As a deer longs for flowing streams,
so longs my soul for you, O God.
My soul thirsts for God,
for the living God.
When shall I come and behold the face of God?

Psalm 42:1–2

CHAPTER 5

The Merciful

*Blessed are the merciful, for they
shall obtain mercy.*

MATTHEW 5:7

"I Forgive You"

In June of 2015, I was living on the Charleston peninsula as the priest-director of a Catholic residence for men. The city of Charleston is an enchanting place. While busy, it's still relatively quiet. It's the type of city where you can still walk downtown, have a nice meal, and greet a stranger without any serious worries. The city is oftentimes called the "Holy City" since every few blocks has a church and the city's skyline is decorated by the spirals of steeples. God is publicly honored, and religion is revered as a part of the city's fabric of life. As a consequence, quoting many locals, "No one messes with a church."

This was true until the evening of June 17, 2015, when a young man entered the Mother Emanuel AME Church off Marion Square, near the sprawling campus of the College of Charleston. When he entered the house of worship, several members of the congregation were conducting a Bible study.

They may have innocently suspected that he was a summer college student or just a young person looking for direction and guidance. He was warmly welcomed, and the pastor, who was facilitating the Bible study, invited the young man to approach him and sit next to him. It's worth noting that the last act of this shepherd was to welcome a stranger, someone he didn't know.

After sitting in the study for a little while, the young man—without provocation and with unchecked rage—produced a weapon and began to shoot those around him. It was a scene charged with fear, racism, violence, blood, and confusion. By the end, several were wounded and nine were dead. It was an attack unknown in the Holy City's culture and history. And to the families of the victims, it would be a moment of shock and grief burned into their hearts and memories.

At the time of this tragedy, several other American cities, such as Ferguson and Baltimore, were being torn apart by racial hostility. In the fragile state our country found itself in, how did Charleston respond?

Being led by the Christian legacy of the victims and the witness of their families, Charleston was guided along a different direction. The Holy City reacted with prayer and countered evil with mercy. As authorities searched for the mass shooter, prayer vigils were taking place. And when Dylann Roof, the murderous assailant, was taken into custody, parades for peace and reconciliation were held. The response of the city culminated in Dylann Roof's bond hearing.

During the hearing, the families of the victims each came forward and, in actions that were as surprising as they were civilizing, each one forgave the young man who violently took the lives of their loved ones.

Some of the comments during the hearing, made with choking voices and strong tears, display a radical forgiveness: "You have killed some of the most beautiful people that I know. We welcomed you Wednesday night in our Bible study with open arms. Every fiber in my body hurts. I will never be the same. . . . But, as they say in the Bible study, we enjoyed you—but may God have mercy on your soul," said Felicia Sanders whose twenty-six-year-old son, Tywanza Sanders, was one of the victims.

"Although my grandfather and the other victims died at the hands of hate, this is proof that they lived in love. Hate won't win," said Alanna Simmons, granddaughter of retired pastor Daniel Simmons.

"I just want everyone to know I forgive you. You took something very precious away from me. I will never get to talk to her ever again. I will never be able to hold her again, but I forgive you. . . . You hurt me. You hurt a lot of people. But God forgive you, and I forgive you," said Nadine Collier, the daughter of seventy-year-old Ethel Lance.

"We are the family that love built. We have no room for hate, so we have to forgive," said Bethane Middleton-Brown. Her forty-nine-year-old sister, Rev. Depayne Middleton, was killed in the attack.

And Anthony Thompson, the grandson of fifty-nine-year-old Myra Thompson, said, "We would like you to take this opportunity to repent. Repent. Confess. Give your life to the One who matters the most, Jesus Christ, so he can change your ways, no matter what happens to you, and you'll be okay."

The bond hearing was a city-wide and national Christian witness to the power of mercy. The families of the victims were as human as each of us. These weren't easy acts of mercy. They weren't comfortable or taken lightly. The mercy was severe. It required the strength of their faith. These believers knew they were the recipients of a tender mercy from God and were therefore strengthened and urged to give this mercy to Dylann Roof. As they desired true happiness, they knew that mercy was needed; clinging to hate would only tear them down more than they already were. Through their mercy, the city of Charleston—veiled in mourning—saw hate and anger vanquished by clemency and kindness. The city saw the light of happiness emerge from tremendous darkness.

This type of healing, hope, and peace is what can happen in cities, work places, parishes, families, and marriages that are bold enough to seek mercy and bountifully share it with others. To those who give mercy, mercy becomes a way of life and a sure path to happiness.

Mercy and Love

An essential understanding of God in both the Old and New Testaments is that he is all-loving, all-forgiving, and all-merciful. In Jesus Christ, we also see that God is all-happiness. In these disclosures of himself, God shows us the inner power of mercy and its necessity in our lives if we choose to be happy. As Existence and Power itself, God constantly chooses mercy. Each of us who are his children—made in his image—should also willingly choose mercy. But what does it mean to be merciful?

In the Sacred Scriptures, the notion of mercy is a profound concept involving many layers of meaning far beyond the removal of guilt. In the Old Testament, the Hebrew word *hesed* could mean "kindness," "love," "tenderness," "compassion," "acceptance," and "mercy"; therefore, in most places in the Old Testament, when we see the word *mercy*, it could just as well be translated as "kindness" or "love." The same word is used because it assumes an intimate relationship between two people or parties of people, and in doing so, it encompasses all the aspects of such a relationship. Generally summarized, however, the word *hesed* is usually translated as "loving kindness."

The use of a predominantly singular word in these different ways blatantly shows us that, for the Bible, mercy is about relationship. It's cushioned between the kindness and tenderness exchanged between people who care about each other. Mercy is given to us by God because he loves us; therefore, we are called to give mercy to others because we love them. This love could be benevolent and given to someone simply because they belong to the same human race, or our love could be more endearing because someone is a member of our family, a friend, or a close neighbor.

In conclusion, we could say that, for the Bible, mercy is more about a living room than a courtroom. It's more about a father's love than a judge's gavel. In these ways, mercy shows the human family that love is more powerful than betrayal, and grace is always stronger than sin.

In understanding the broader rapport between love and mercy, we can now define mercy's specific role in relationships. Mercy is a loving kindness that forgives a fault or an offense, leaving both parties far better off, both the one who was guilty of the offense and the one who was offended. Mercy's loving kindness provides the offender with the forum for accepting his or her fault and the freedom to change his or her life, while also freeing the offended from painful consequences (the "side effects" if you will) that always come from vengeance, resentment, and anger. Mercy gives the victim an independence from the offense and provides the offender with the liberty to convert and begin a new path.

But of course, mercy does not just go hand in hand with love; it also has another counterpart that is immensely important in how we understand mercy.

Mercy and Justice

Mercy is harmoniously united to justice. Rather than opposed to one another, mercy and justice both work together for the holistic flourishing of the human person and society. In order for mercy to be substantial, therefore, it must fulfill justice. If justice is ignored, then mercy is not present. In such a situation, licentious behavior, irresponsibility, and foolishness are disguised as mercy. If mercy is ignored, then justice is not present. In such a scenario, vengeance, resentment, and rage are inaccurately identified as justice. As St. Thomas Aquinas taught: "Mercy without justice is the mother of dissolution. Justice without mercy is cruelty."

This last point needs to be developed since many contemporary depictions of justice are exaggerated and inaccurate. Justice is a noble virtue—one that should be esteemed—since it teaches us what is properly due to another person or society. Whether justice is teaching children how to treat a neighbor's yard with respect, a citizen joining the army to defend his homeland, or the repayment of a financial debt, it is the basis of civilization and civic friendship. When exercised properly, it is always accompanied by prudence, temperance, and fortitude.

Vengeance, however, is a distortion of justice since it exaggerates what is appropriately due to someone. This exaggerated response can be expressed in both an active or passive way.

Vengeance can be passive in a dismissive manner that completely negates the existence, goodness, or well-being of another person. It's as if the person did not or does not exist. It's summarized by the popular exclamation "Go to hell" but is sincerely meant and is heightened by a true lack of care or concern for the other person. For example, this can be seen in a family member who totally cuts off a loved one because of a hurt or offense. No overtures of mercy or reconciliation are ever offered or even considered. It's as if the person is dead and the one exercising such vengeance is content with this perception.

Vengeance can also be expressed in an active way that desires the total annihilation of the person, his reputation, goodness, and well-being. The one who has given the hurt or offense is made to pay dearly by counterattacks and animosity from the one exercising vengeance. This active expression is seen in the fearful command "I will rain hellfire upon you!" The example used a moment ago to show passive vengeance can also be applied here, just in the other direction. Picture the offended family member reciprocating the offense in an intensified manner. They continue to attack the loved one until they see real harm or devastating consequences. They want the person to bleed or grovel and take sick pleasure in seeing these results.

In either version, vengeance diminishes or destroys the person and dismantles the civility of society. This is not justice. In true form, justice edifies a person and builds up the common good of a society and culture. Mercy fulfills justice and offers a person and a people a reformed way of life more in accordance with goodness and virtue.

And so some immediate questions might arise. If mercy fulfills justice, does this imply that mercy accepts the role of discipline? Shouldn't mercy absolve discipline and consequences?

Mercy, Accountability, and Discipline

Mercy calls a person to accept the consequences of their actions and to embrace the discipline that comes with them. The contemporary term *discipline* is what the Bible means by "punishment." While not enjoyable, it's welcomed by a person who wants to be virtuous, happy, and holy.

This clarification might be surprising to some since many contemporary views falsely define mercy as a clean slate without accountability or consequences. This is not mercy. In order to be true and substantial—a help to the person and society—mercy must fulfill justice. To dismiss a person's accountability is to cause harm to the person's own call to goodness and virtue. For mercy to be a path of reform, justice must discipline and admonish the person about the consequences of vice and darkness; this way, the path of goodness is understood, desired, and pursued. Any supposed mercy without justice is misplaced and is irresponsible compassion. It fails to teach and guide the person to a true reform of life and could enable a bad act to become a bad habit.

After the attempted assassination of Pope St. John Paul II, the pontiff visited his would-be assassin in the jail where he was detained. The two spoke person-to-person and John Paul forgave him. After their conversation, the Holy Father left the jail, but the man had to remain. For the pope's mercy to be legitimate, justice had to be served. The would-be assassin had to accept society's discipline for this offense to the pope and the common good. This helps us to understand the dynamics between mercy and justice and the role of discipline.

In terms of discipline, therefore, justice is always reasonable. It's regularly assisted by prudence, temperance, and fortitude.

Temperance examines justice to assure that it does not slide into vengeance. It helps justice to be proportionate, which means the discipline matches the offense. We cannot treat a profane word the same way we would a physical attack. A child who steals a cookie for an evening snack should not be disciplined in the same way as a teenager who has snuck out of the house to drink with friends. Again, good discipline matches the offense. It's tempered and reasonable.

Prudence helps justice in evaluating the circumstances of the offense, the intention of the offender, and the level of his repentance. If someone steals bread because of their own starvation or to help another famished person, they should not be disciplined in the same way as the person who steals out of indulgence or greed. Circumstances can never justify an unlawful act, but they should be considered in what discipline is given.

In so many different cases, prudence assists justice by helping fulfill its role to teach the person about what is right and good. To the degree that a particular act bears some aspect of goodness in its intention, justice acknowledges it and seeks to "reward it" with a lighter discipline. True justice never squashes goodness, however thin, and it never extinguishes even the smallest flame of righteousness in the person.

In particular, prudence assesses the degree of an offender's repentance. This is a delicate task but one that is most necessary. If someone is truly repentant, then discipline should be lighter since its task is to affirm and strengthen what is good. If the offender is insincere or lacking repentance, then justice must be more strict and severe; it must since it seeks the authentic good of the person and the well-being and safety of society.

If someone were to violate a confidence by repeating private information but afterward show deep repentance, then a friend should be light in whatever discipline is given. Perhaps after a few days to cool down, the offended friend might accept reconciliation with the one who hurt him. But if someone else were to inflict the same harm and show no repentance or even seek to justify the offense, then the discipline could be greater, even to the degree of avoiding reconciliation. And so the level of a person's repentance does not justify an offense, but it is deeply considered in deciding what discipline should be given.

Or consider a wife who is the victim of domestic violence and finally leaves her abusive husband. There is little chance, if any at all, that they will reconcile their marriage (and they probably shouldn't in most cases). But she may still be able to forgive him after some time passes and perhaps after some pastoral counseling. This mercy does not justify the horrible sins of the husband; it still acknowledges the evil that was done, while at the same time brings about the healing of the deep wounds suffered by both parties. Mercy will free them both.

In each situation, though reconciliation may not be possible, mercy should still be extended since our own freedom from the offense depends upon it. The degree of mercy may depend on their intention and sincerity of repentance, but only darkness can live within the souls of the merciless. We must avoid the misery that comes from clinging to bitterness. As people of good will and believers in Jesus Christ, we must seek the legitimate good of the other person.

Lastly, justice is assisted by fortitude, which empowers it when it runs the risk of being overwhelmed by emotion. Fortitude gives justice strength to move above our passions and seek the help of reason. It calls justice to greater knowledge and perception. Fortitude is a tremendous help to justice in a culture moved by emotion and oftentimes lacking in serious discernment or due process.

A Lived Example

All of these explanations can get confusing. It may help to apply everything to a relatively common occurrence in most families. Picture a child being told that he cannot have dessert after dinner, but he disobeys and eats a cookie in his bed. In the morning, his mother sees the cookie crumbs. This act of disobedience hurts not only the child but the moral health and common good of the family.

The mother has two options in terms of retribution. First, she could see the crumbs, clean them up, and never mention anything to the child. This would be a passive vengeance since it ignores the child and nurtures vice in him. This sort of reaction is born from possible sentiments within the parent. "I don't have time for this." "I've told him not to do this before and it's just not worth the trouble; I've got to pick my battles." "I don't care. Whatever." And similar such reactions.

Or she sees the crumbs, violently pulls the child into the room, screams and yells, punches the wall, and rips the covers off the bed in a fit of rage. Obviously, this is active vengeance since it causes fear and seeks to harm the person, if not physically, then psychologically.

Beyond these two dramatically different options is a level-headed response that lies somewhere in the middle. The mother can choose mercy and welcome a measured form of justice at the same time. She could call the child into the room and calmly ask about the crumbs, doing her best to practice temperance, prudence, and fortitude. She'll temper her resolutions on discipline until she hears the child's explanation (and hopeful confession). Her prudence helps her assess the situation and ask the right questions to help her understand what was going on in the child's mind when he disobeyed (to hopefully help him curb future behavior away from this mindset). And her fortitude helps her keep her cool, especially if she is already tired and frustrated from the other demands of the day.

If the child acknowledges that he broke a rule and shows repentance, then her discipline might be light; there will be a gentle rebuke and explanation of why disobeying is wrong. The child has to apologize and clean up the crumbs.

If the child enters the room and willfully lies, denying that he broke the rule and blaming a sibling, then discipline must be more serious. While still being cautious not to fall into vengeance, justice must be firm in this situation. Perhaps the child has to clean the bed and is not able to have desserts for a week. The idea is to have a consistent reaction to the behavior of the child when he is confronted. Whatever is within the realm of temperance, prudence, and fortitude can be exercised by the parent so that the child will be led to virtue.

The above example, however trivial or ordinary it might be, can help us all to understand the rapport between mercy and justice. In greater or more emotional situations, it would be helpful for us to remember this dynamic and to respond to offenses with loving kindness.

We must remember that justice needs temperance, prudence, and fortitude in order to be reasonable. Likewise, mercy needs justice in order to be substantial and helpful to us and to society. Mercy never tells a person that their offense is acceptable, nor does it give unreasonable excuses; rather, it welcomes justice and its discipline, and it calls the offender to accountability, repentance, and a reform of life. Reform of life is the primary purpose of mercy. Euphoric emotions, psychological self-esteem, and warm feelings are helpful, but they are not the intention of mercy. The purpose of mercy, assisted by justice, is to help us become a better person for ourselves and our loved ones, a more benevolent citizen to our society, and a stronger believer and lover of God. In these ways, mercy helps us to be happy.

The Good Thief

In his Gospel account, St. Luke describes Jesus's crucifixion and the two thieves flanking Our Lord who shared a similar fate on Golgotha. One scoffed at him like the Roman guards, saying, "Are you not the Christ? Save yourself and us!" (Lk 23:39). The mockery questioned his divinity and verbally abused him as he also endured physical sufferings on the cross.

The other thief, however, broke the cycle of abuse and admonished his fellow prisoner: "Do you not fear God, since you are under the same sentence of condemnation? And we indeed justly; for we are receiving the due reward of our deeds; but this man has done nothing wrong" (Lk 23:40–41). And then, dismissing himself from the darkness around him, the man took a leap toward mercy. Broken and actively dying, the thief repented, asking the Lord, "Jesus, remember me when you come in your kingly power" (v. 42). To the one now appropriately called the "good thief," the Lord unselfishly and lavishly poured out his mercy upon him, saying, "Truly, I say to you, today you will be with me in Paradise" (v. 43).

This example from the Lord's passion teaches us two primary lessons. First, the kindness shown to the good thief displays for all humanity how much God truly loves each one of us and is willing to do anything or go anywhere in order to seek us out and bring us back to divine fellowship. Secondly, the mercy shown to the good thief gives credibility to the assertion that with God, all sincere acts of repentance and requests for heaven are heard and answered by the Lord Jesus, no matter the gravity of the offense or the depravity of the offender.

The unrepentant thief, however, reminds us of the path of misery that we will walk if we fuel our resentment, anger, and violence. As the wicked thief does not seek mercy, so mercy and its benefits, such as happiness, cannot be received or enjoyed.

A Murderer-Turned-Apostle

As mercy is shown to one person, so mercy is forwarded to others. This was the case for the great apostle St. Paul, also known as Saul. This man was formerly a persecutor of Christians who would go to any length to ensure their destruction. We know that he was involved or presided over the deaths of many (cf. Acts 9:1). For example, Paul was present in the stoning of the first Christian martyr, St. Stephen. During his martyrdom, Stephen prayed, "Lord Jesus, receive my spirit," and, "Lord, do not hold this sin against them" (Acts 7:59–60). The spiritual masters have always considered Paul's encounter with the Lord Jesus to be the fruit of Stephen's prayers. Thus, we see that Stephen's petition for mercy won the conversion of Paul.

And so the zealous Paul was "knocked off his high horse." Jesus came to him on his way to Damascus, just after he left Stephen's martyrdom, as a flash of light. Paul was thrown to the ground and the Lord asked him, "Saul, Saul, why do you persecute me?" (Acts 9:4).

Not understanding what was happening, Saul asked, "Who are you, Lord?" The response was clear: "I am Jesus, whom you are persecuting; but rise and enter the city, and you will be told what you are to do" (Acts 9:5–6).

The brilliance of the Lord's flash of light blinded Paul. He was suddenly a broken man. He entered Damascus as he was told and stayed there for three days. God sent him Ananias, who preached the Good News to him. Paul repented and received baptism. At that moment, scales fell from his eyes and his sight was restored. God not only gave him his physical eyesight but—through his mercy—also opened the eyes of his heart. Paul was so shaken by these experiences that he went to the desert of Arabia and spent time in prayer and reflection (Gal 1:17).

God's mercy brought about Paul's conversion, radically changed his life, and made him a new creation. Paul would declare, "For I through the law died to the law, that I might live to God. I have been crucified with Christ; it is no longer

I who live, but Christ who lives in me; and the life I now live in the flesh I live by faith in the Son of God, who loved me and gave himself for me" (Gal 2:19–20).

And, having received mercy, he was called to share and announce it: "So we are ambassadors for Christ, God making his appeal through us. We beg you on behalf of Christ, be reconciled to God" (2 Cor 5:20).

This summons to share the message of mercy led the apostle on three apostolic voyages throughout the Mediterranean world. As he formed and nurtured Christian communities, he wrote several letters that are now part of the New Testament. These include letters to the Romans, Corinthians, Galatians, Philippians, Ephesians, Colossians, and Thessalonians, as well as pastoral letters to Timothy and Titus and on behalf of Philemon.

Converted by mercy, St. Paul lived his life for Jesus Christ and, in the end, offered his life as an oblation, dying by beheading in Rome. A once-persecutor of God's people became a shepherd to them and a witness to the power of God's mercy to change lives and bestow happiness on even the most unlikely of souls.

All of this proves that God's mercy is for everyone and, when accepted, great things can happen. God's redemptive power is mighty, and to those who accept and share it, he can bring about the most unexpected, creative, and wonderful conversions, restorations, miracles, and signs of goodness.

Tears of Mercy

In the Lord Jesus's public ministry, there was an unusual circumstance that led to a manifestation of great forgiveness and mercy.

Simon, a Pharisee, had invited Jesus to his home for dinner. The man welcomed Jesus but suspended the usual displays of hospitality. The Lord took a seat at the table, and during the meal, a sinful woman believed to be a prostitute, entered the home uninvited, approached Jesus with confidence and gently washed his feet with her tears (see Lk 7:36–50).

The woman then brushed over the tears with her hair and bathed his feet with perfume. Simon and the other dinner guests were appalled that Jesus would allow a sinner like this woman to touch him and care for him. Jesus reacts to the criticisms by telling a story: "A certain creditor has two debtors; one owed five hundred denarii, and the other fifty. When they could not pay, he forgave them both. Now which of them will love him more?" (Lk 7:41–42).

Simon responded that the one with the larger debt would love the moneylender more. Jesus affirmed that Simon gave the correct answer. Then he began to admonish Simon for his lack of love and attention to him: "Do you see this woman? I entered your house, you gave me no water for my feet, but she has wet my feet with her tears and wiped them with her hair. You gave me no kiss, but from the time I came in she has not ceased to kiss my feet. You did not anoint my head with oil, but she has anointed my feet with ointment" (Lk 7:44–46).

And then the Lord showed his gratitude by responding to the woman's unspoken plea: "Therefore I tell you, her sins, which are many, are forgiven, for she loved much; but he who is forgiven little, loves little" (Lk 7:47).

The sinful woman washed and kissed Jesus's feet and showed in her actions the sorrow and repentance she felt in her heart. The Lord recognized her love, however blurred by sin, and tenderly said to her, "Your sins are forgiven" (Lk 7:48).

In the encounter with this woman and his display of mercy, Jesus shows each of us that through sincere contrition, expressed in words and works, mercy and compassion are available to all of us. Even if society will not welcome us or others are hardened in their lack of compassion toward us, we can always approach Jesus. He will never reject us and always desires to heal and forgive us. We must simply have the humility and confidence to draw near to him.

Mount to Mission

In order to be happy, we must live a life of mercy. No one can be happy while holding (while greedily storing up) resentment or anger in their hearts. We must let our scars and wounds go and release their burdens from our souls.

Though it seems impossible after someone has caused us pain, it is necessary for our happiness that we forgive them. This forgiveness ensures our freedom from the slavery of bitterness, but it is also an act of charity to our offenders as we sincerely seek their own freedom and conversion.

Forgiveness takes strength. It's not pity, but real compassion (which is a word that comes from the Latin words meaning "to suffer with"). Forgiveness involves suffering because we take on the sorrows of another's sin. This is why compassion and mercy require emotional strength to toss aside pride, anger, and other sins.

At times, it may seem that offenders are given greater mercy than the righteous, but this is a reward from God to the righteous; namely, that he allows the righteous to suffer for the sake of the unrighteous in imitation of Jesus Christ and his saving work. It further humbles those seeking righteousness as they realize that, at times, they are the ones in need of mercy and compassion. To any person stuck in sin, God shows deeper compassion since they are the ones most in need of his mercy. It takes the strength and witness of the righteous to encourage and lead the sinner to repentance.

Being merciful is also being a person of justice. We do the work of God in forgiving others because it is just. God wants justice for sinners because it ultimately leads to their salvation (the justice of purgatory literally leads right to our salvation in heaven). When we forgive a sinner and show mercy, we are allowing God to continue his work in us and in them. When we avoid vengeance toward a sinner, we open a path to the person's redemption. This might one day be a path that we ourselves will need from others.

In forgiving, we avoid rash judgment and slander. We should not speak ill of those who have offended or hurt us or seek violence toward them, no matter what we feel in the passion of the moment they have sinned against us. Jesus constantly defends sinners and honors their wish for forgiveness, and strongly opposes anyone who tries to discourage or harm them. The Lord calls us all to an examination of our own conscience and a sober knowledge of ourselves. As he taught us all: "Why do you see the speck that is in your brother's eye, but do not notice the log that is in your own eye?" (Mt 7:3).

As we look at the intricacies, challenges, and dynamism of mercy and compassion, justice and discipline, a few examples from everyday life might help us. We can see:

- The mother who forgives her child for misbehaving in a store and gives a tempered discipline to him even though she's embarrassed and upset.

- The employee barked at by his boss knows that his boss is normally a good person and is under pressure on a new project, and so forgives the man and gently brings it up later.

- The family that is under financial pressure and plans a yard sale. The night before, someone steals their yard sale items, and rather than responding with rage, they pray for the unknown person, complete a police report, and look for other ways to bring money into their home.

- The store owner who catches a would-be thief realizes the food was being stolen because of hunger and offers the person a chance to sweep the store and receive the food they need.

- The wife who feels neglected by her husband and is inclined to bitterness but sees the darkness in her own heart, repents, forgives her husband, and sits down to talk with him, using temperance and prudence to address her grievances and concerns.

- The teenager who sneaks out of the house one night, hangs out with friends, and returns home. He sees the love and trust his parents have for him the next day, is moved by sorrow, and confesses to them what he did and is willing to accept the appropriate discipline.

In living with a merciful spirit that seeks and gives forgiveness, we pursue happiness and enrich our lives and the lives of those around us. In being merciful, we receive mercy and find greater strength to be compassionate, kind, patient, and tender toward others, especially those who have offended or hurt us or a loved one.

As we grow in mercy, we find a love for prayer and are consoled by our time with God. Our prayer becomes more about being like God and less about what we want. In these ways, we grow in our awareness, acceptance, and appreciation of mercy and love.

Examination of Conscience

- Do I hold grudges and feed resentment toward others?
- Am I inclined to rash judgment or unattainable expectations toward my neighbor?
- Do I regularly go to confession and repent of my sins to God?
- Do I humble myself and ask for mercy when I have offended or hurt someone?
- Am I willing to accept appropriate discipline for my offenses?
- Do I find myself angry due to stubbornness and an unwillingness to forgive?
- Am I generous in my mercy to others? Do I pray for sinners?
- Do I fuel greed or envy in my life and in my dealings with others?
- Do I actively fight against sin in my life and in the lives of those under my charge?
- Do I temperately give discipline to those who have offended or hurt me?

School of Discipleship

Continuing in the School of Discipleship, it is now time to look at the fifth beatitude: **the merciful.**

When we show mercy to others, the Holy Spirit bestows us with the gift of **counsel**. Mercy cultivates within us a compassionate and loving spirit. If we offer mercy to someone who is suffering, whether it be physical, emotional, or spiritual, we are able to bring them counsel and make them feel better. Just as we may guide a person away from sin or instruct them on how to deal with emotional trauma, so the Holy Spirit, in fulfilling the promise of this beatitude that we too will be shown mercy, comes to us and gives us his counsel, which enlightens us to do and say the right thing in the face of trials.

Once we receive this gift, the virtue of **prudence** is perfected in our soul. As we engage the hearts of others through counsel, we are led to prudently accompany our neighbor. Just as fortitude in the last chapter allowed us to act courageously, here, the counsel we "take in" from the Holy Spirit allows us to act prudently; or said another way, it enables us to be careful in our decisions and what we say. The *Catechism* says prudence is "the virtue that disposes practical reason to discern our true good in every circumstance and to choose the right means of achieving it" (CCC 1806).

This beatitude, gift, and virtue help us to better understand the petition in the Lord's Prayer **"And forgive us our trespasses, as we forgive those who trespass against us."** This bears a clear connection to acting with mercy and being shown mercy, as forgiveness goes hand in hand with mercy. The blossoming of this petition leads us to the promise of this beatitude, which is to be shown mercy. If we show mercy to others (if we forgive them their trespasses), we will be the beneficiary of God's mercy (he will forgive our trespasses).

Lastly, the path that begins from this beatitude and crosses through these other aspects of the spiritual life helps us to recognize the hoarding and darkness of the capital sin of **greed**. One might think that the opposite of mercy is anger or envy, and while these vices are opposed to mercy, the actual opposite of mercy is greed. With greed, we usually think in materialistic terms; we conjure of a Gordon Gekko kind of figure, a money-hungry Wall Street tycoon. But this anti-beatitude can be seen principally in the context of our emotions and the movement of our hearts. Mercy is about being completely selfless, open, and free, whereas greed is self-absorbed, closed-in, and enslaved to its passions, emotions, and desires.

The person entrenched in greed is focused more on their own importance than on a genuine openness and care of others. A greedy person will not share happiness, love, or mercy. He will stay angry over an offense and burden the happiness of others. Greed relishes grudges and digs deeper pits of animosity toward others. It cannot let go of a hurt and bounces between resentment and self-pity on one hand, and manipulation and deception on the other. Just like the material greed of the Wall Street tycoon wants to collect as much worldly treasure as possible, the spiritually greedy want to collect grudges and animosity and store them up in a "bank" of ill-will.

Those trapped in greed become strangers to themselves. They pity the poor but do not offer any assistance. They judge offenses but never ask for forgiveness. They envy the happy but don't seek happiness themselves. As greed desperately seeks to hoard, it only empties our hearts even more. Left to its own devices, greed will black out the light of goodness in our hearts and lead us down a path of misery, bitterness, and hatred.

As the promise of the merciful is to receive mercy, so the punishment of the anti-beatitude is an empty and bitter heart. The greedy many who collects earthly wealth and does not share it will not be given charity if he loses all that he has; in the same way, one who does not offer mercy will not receive it himself when he is in need.

In conclusion, the fifth row of our spiritual matrix looks like this:

BEATITUDE	GIFT OF THE SPIRIT	CORRESPONDING VIRTUE	PETITION OF THE LORD'S PRAYER	CAPITAL SIN/ ANTI-BEATITUDE
Blessed are the merciful, for they shall obtain mercy	Counsel	Prudence	And forgive us our trespasses as we forgive those who trespass against us	Greed

Prayer

Generous Father,
I want to be merciful and happy.
Give me your strength and guidance.
Keep greed far from my heart. Teach me compassion.
Help me to see the sufferings and sorrows of others.
Never let me hold a grudge or be unjust to others.
Come to me, Father, and give me prudence.
Bring me into your kingdom! Show me happiness.
Through Christ our Lord. Amen.

Three Helpful Truths to be Merciful:

+ I am a sinner who is loved and has been forgiven.

+ Seeing the heart of the one who has offended me, I need to remind myself that they are a well-beloved child of God.

+ In my life, I need to pay forward and generously give the mercy that I have received.

The Command of the Lord Jesus

Jesus looked up and said to her, "Woman, where are they? Has no one condemned you?" She said, "No one, Lord." And Jesus said, "Neither do I condemn you; go, and do not sin again."

John 8:10–11

The Psalmist's Prayer

Out of the depths I cry to you, O Lord!
Lord, hear my voice!
Let your ears be attentive to the voice of my supplications!
If you, O Lord, should mark iniquities,
Lord, who could stand?
But there is forgiveness with you, that you may be feared.
I wait for the Lord, my soul waits,
and in his word I hope;
My soul waits for the Lord
more than watchmen for the morning,
more than watchmen for the morning.
O Israel, hope in the Lord!
For with the Lord there is mercy,
and with him is plenteous redemption.
And he will redeem Israel from all his iniquities.

Psalm 130

— CHAPTER 6 —

PURE IN HEART

*Blessed are the pure in heart, for
they shall see God.*

MATTHEW 5:8

A Virgin Martyr

In the fall of 2015, the body of St. Maria Goretti was brought
to the United States for the first time. Since the Second World
War, this little saint has endeared herself to the American people. The affection began when US troops were encamped
near her shrine in Nettuno after the Battle of Anzio. While
stationed there, soldiers frequently asked for the intercession
of the virgin-martyr for their safety, purity, and perseverance.
After the war, many soldiers brought the story and devotion
of Maria Goretti to North America.

During the saint's tour, thousands of people in multiple
cities turned out to pray to St. Maria Goretti and pay her
homage. At the time of the martyr's visit, my ministry as a
priest involved a parish and a school. In the mornings, I would
teach religion to the eighth graders. From the generosity of
certain benefactors, arrangements were made for my students

to go see the little saint at Holy Spirit Church in Atlanta, Georgia. Leading up to their pilgrimage, the eighth graders studied the life and witness of Maria, and their excitement grew as they realized they would soon be able to see her body and pray in front of her reliquary.

During our time in Atlanta, I was inspired by the devotion of the middle schoolers as they approached the body and offered their prayers. Like so many Americans, each of these students found a special heavenly friend in Maria Goretti.

What is it about this little saint that has inspired so many people over these past several decades? What can this martyr of purity teach us about happiness?

Maria Goretti grew up in a poor, hard-working, and faith-filled family. They didn't have much, but there was love, virtue, and deep prayer. Maria's father had to move the family because of work, and when he died from malaria, he left the family with two questionable characters, a father and son who lived on the same property to share the workload. But these two men were difficult and even dangerous, taking advantage of the now-fatherless family by using the widow and her children as servants in the fields and kitchen.

Maria was always seen as a happy person with a pure heart. She tried to help neighbors with their chores and would often give away extra eggs or vegetables to those in need. Maria always went the extra mile in service to her mother and took care of her younger siblings with tenderness and kindness. The young girl had a great attentiveness to the needs of others and took care of her duties with a noticeable innocence and selflessness.

Maria was also a girl of keen reverence for God. After her first Holy Communion, when she heard some of the other

children making impure jokes, she was completely shocked
and outraged. How could anyone say such things and still
receive Holy Communion? Her purity was not prudishness
or disguised fear. It was a passionate love for Jesus Christ that
would not allow anything to diminish or blemish it. It saw
the horror of sin and chose the purity and beauty of holiness
every day.

Alessandro Serenelli, the son in the duo living with the
Goretti family, also saw our saint's gentleness of soul. Addicted
to control and lustful pleasure, he wanted Maria for himself
and made two advances on her. At first, Maria did not understand, but then she realized what Alessandro was suggesting.
She refused him both times, telling him that it was a sin. She
was calling the young man to a purity of heart.

Alessandro was angered by Maria's responses. On July 5,
1902, while everyone else was in the fields working, Maria
was taking care of the house duties and watching her young-
est sibling. While the child slept, Alessandro approached Maria
and began to sexually harass her. Maria screamed and fought.
In radical opposition to the destructive sin of lust, and with
the boldness of a saint, Maria told Alessandro, "No! No! I will
not! I will not! It is a sin, God forbids it. You will go to hell,
Alessandro. You will go to hell if you do it." Even in moments
of immediate danger, Maria was more worried about God's
majesty and Alessandro's soul than for her own safety and
well-being.

Alessandro would not be dissuaded. In his rage, he showed
her a knife and warned Maria, "Give in or die!" With a res-
olution of her purity of heart and a burning love for Jesus
Christ, little Maria roared like a lion, "No, I will not! No! It is
a sin!" Alessandro lunged at Maria and began to viciously stab

her fourteen times. She fell on the floor bloody and wounded as her attacker fled the scene. Maria's mother and neighbors hurried to her as they heard her screams. In seeing the condition of her body, they were surprised that she was still alive. Immediately, she was hurried to the hospital a few towns over.

In the last few hours of her life, when the priest came to administer the Last Rites, he asked her, "And you, Maria, do you pardon your murderer?" Little Maria, dying and in great pain, said to the priest, "Yes, for the love of Jesus, I pardon him. And I desire that he may come with me to heaven."

This declaration of forgiveness reflected the purity of Maria's heart. Even as she lay dying as a victim of a horrible assault, she could see goodness in Alessandro and wished salvation upon him. Maria sought no vengeance, wanted no evil, and spoke no curses. She loved with a pure heart, welcomed grace, and remained a light in the midst of darkness.

Alessandro was eventually caught and taken immediately to jail. He denied that he was involved in the attack on Maria and then claimed to be out of his mind. His attempts to avoid accountability, however, were without success. After a trial, during which he was both foul and offensive in his demeanor, he was sentenced to thirty years in prison. In the first few years of prison, his heart remained hard, showing no remorse for his sins against Maria.

Alessandro's cynicism enslaved him. He was under a dark cloud of despair and guilt, but mercy would prevail. The very one whose life he took would come to him and help him save his own.

One evening in a dream, Maria came to Alessandro dressed in white, barefooted, and beaming with great joy. She was walking in a field of lilies and handed several of them to

Alessandro. Hesitantly, he received them. As he did, the lilies became tongues of fire. He was confused and looked at Maria. She simply smiled and he woke up.

Once awake, Alessandro knew exactly what the dream meant. He understood that the lilies were symbols of innocence that were now being offered to him again, while the tongues of fire were symbols of a purgation that he would need to undergo in order to be restored to a life of grace.

That very night Alessandro turned to Jesus Christ and begged for mercy. We can imagine Maria rejoicing with the heavenly host over the conversion of this sinner! Her mercy, love, and self-control stand as a bright reflection of a pure heart in the midst of a fallen world. Through the toils of life and the offense of an assailant, Maria looked for goodness and showed kindness to all. She shows us that a purity of heart involves bodily chastity, but also a spiritual temperance, compassion, and a generous spirit open even to the most wayward souls. In this way, the pure of heart are able to see God. This is the path to happiness and the life we are all called to live as the children of God.

What Is the Heart?

When God made man and woman, he established us as the crown of his creation. He molded our hearts for happiness and freedom so that we could know him and discern his presence, love him and imitate him, and so worship him and share fellowship with him in this life and into eternity. Our hearts, therefore, require purity, an absence of sin, so that it can pursue God and his goodness.

But what is the biblical notion of the heart? Obviously, it

more than just the physical organ responsible for the movement of blood throughout our bodies. And, yes, while certainly more is intended than mere biology, it should be noted that it's precisely because of the function and the importance of the physical heart that the Bible uses it as such a sacred image. As the physical heart moves blood throughout our bodies, so the spiritual heart moves grace and goodness throughout our souls.

With this understanding, what more is intended by the word "heart"? In the Bible, the heart is the dwelling-place where we reside with ourselves; it's where each of us "lives." It is the place to which we can withdraw in moments of reflection, joy, or sorrow. Spiritually, the heart is seen as our hidden center. It has reasons beyond the grasp of our minds, and according to biblical wisdom, it is only the Spirit of God that can plumb the depths of our heart. As the prophet Jeremiah teaches: "The heart is deceitful above all things, and desperately corrupt; who can understand it? I the Lord search the mind and test the heart, to give to every man according to his ways, according to the fruit of his doings" (Jer 17:9–10).

And St. Paul confirms the role of the Holy Spirit: "For what person knows a man's thoughts except the spirit of the man which is in him? So also no one comprehends the thoughts of God except the Spirit of God" (1 Cor 2:11).

Perhaps it is best to say the heart is the place of *decision*. It's where we encounter God and choose him, and where we renew our covenant with him. The heart is the crucible, the crossroad, and the place of conversion. In order for it to help us see God, our heart must be pure. Such purity begins with a freedom from sin and an attraction to evil and darkness.

Love's Power

A pure heart includes chaste affections and desires, a custody of our mind and will, and a reverence toward our bodies and the bodies of others.

What makes these pure is not just the absence of sin but also the transparency, kindness, and self-donation of love for God and our neighbor. When exercised selflessly, love purifies and orders our intellect, will, and emotions to God's goodness. Love allows our affections and desires to mature and disciplines our bodies according to virtue. The world often misrepresents love, but St. John clarifies it for us: "By this we know love, that he laid down his life for us; and we ought to lay down our lives for the brethren" (1 Jn 3:16).

Building off this, St. Paul gives a most excellent description of love: "Love is patient, love is kind; love is not jealous or boastful; it is not arrogant or rude. Love does not insist on its own way; it is not irritable or resentful; it does not rejoice at wrong, but rejoices in the right. Love bears all things, believes all things, hopes all things, endures all things" (1 Cor 13:4–7).

Understanding this definition of love helps us cultivate a pure heart, which we must have if we want to see God in the midst of our broken world and confused culture.

Often our affections and desires can challenge the purity of our heart. A sin like lust, which is an inordinate and narcissistic love of pleasure and enjoyment, can kill our purity as it seeks gratification over goodness. Lust betrays beauty in favor of temporary thrills. It is a danger to our ability to see goodness and live a life of love and service to God and others, and it strangles our ability to show mercy and compassion. Lust has led so many down a spiraling path of self-pity, immodesty, anger, disrespect, envy, rash judgment. Perhaps worst of all, though, this sin leads to the objectification of other people.

Therefore, we must practice temperance, always weighing them alongside our relationship with God, our own best good, and the authentic good of our neighbor. We must realize that our desires and affections are not an inviolate standard unto themselves. Simply because we feel something or want something does not make it right or good. Our emotions and inclinations, our attractions and moments of arousal, all require the discernment of our reason and the scrutiny of temperance. These passions can be whimsical and capricious, dark and misguided, so they must be ordered by virtue and directed by faith in God and his divine ordering of all things.

Custody of Our Minds

In addition to our affections and desires, purity of heart also involves *the custody of our minds and the formation of our wills.*

Custody of mind, meaning the ability to focus our thoughts and wills on virtue, relies heavily on prudence since this virtue determines what is right and proper in any number of given situations. Our minds choose our intentions and give reasons for our actions; because of this, they are guided and matured by prudence. As we encounter moments of euphoria, rage, arousal, or other strong emotions and movements of our passions, we are called to order those desires and keep custody of them. This specifically involves a vigilance over our memory and imagination.

Our imagination is a gift given by God. It's meant to enhance our creativity and help us explore ideas beyond time and space. Our imagination can be a tremendous resource to our prayer life and to our efforts to see God's providence in our world today. These positive features of our imagination should be the focus of our energies. We need to avoid using our imagination to create a fantasy world where we are our own gods, where we have delusions of grandeur about fame, money, and sex. Nor can we let our imagination develop plots against other people, develop methods of deception, or objectify other people. These misdirected uses of our imagination can pollute our purity of heart and challenge our ability to be happy. Think about it; if our imagination is focused on painting an unrealistic world that we try to perpetually live in, then our reality will seem dull and unfulfilled and cause us to overlook unfathomable blessings.

Related to our imagination is our memory, which is also a higher ability of our intellect since it reunites us with past things (it helps us re-member them). In this process, such things become a part of us again, a "member" of our person, just as an arm or leg are called "members of the body." Remembering is vastly different from merely recalling some piece of information. We principally have the power to remember so that we can participate in salvation history, especially the sacraments. We also have this ability so that sacred moments in our personal lives and times with our loved ones remain with us beyond spatial-temporal reality. Simply put, our memory helps us to glimpse eternity, as things and moments live on far beyond their actual historical occurrence.

As our memory is a powerful gift and ability, so it relies heavily on fortitude to overcome temptations to abuse it by revisiting old vices, relishing in sinful pleasures from the past, retrieving dark moments of offense, and indulging in previous hurts caused by others. In these ways, our memory can betray our purity of heart. Our desire for happiness, however, will accuse us of these misuses of memory and call us back to the path of goodness and joy.

There is a great story in the monastic tradition that conveys the importance of obtaining custody of our minds. Two monks, one old and the other young, were walking along when they came across a river. There in the currents was a beautiful woman, stuck and in trouble. The old monk offered his help and waded in, carrying her across. The young monk was astonished that his superior would challenge his purity by touching a beautiful woman like this.

When they reached dry land, the woman thanked the old monk and went on her way. As the monks returned to their own journey, the younger one could not get what the old monk did out of his mind. He was scandalized for hours as the two walked along.

Finally, the older monk—after noticing that the younger monk was bothered by something—asked him, "What's wrong?" The young monk said, "I can't believe what you did back there with that woman. It was inappropriate. You carried her across the river! We're monks!"

The older monk smiled and simply replied, "Yes, I did an act of charity. I carried the woman for a few minutes across the river. But what I can't believe is that while I carried her across the river, you have carried her for hours in your heart."

Formation of Our Wills

A purity of heart also requires a formation of our wills, which is the shaping and educating of our ability to make decisions, control our passions, and pursue a proper course of action toward good things. In order for true formation to happen, we have to welcome discipline, fortitude, and chastity. In our lives, we have to be ready to identify certain desires as inappropriate and other affections as inordinate.

We have to nurture an inner fortitude to discern and identify these wayward inclinations so as to defend the purity of our hearts. Such fallen desires can involve a lack of kindness, a restricted generosity, a shallow charity, a refused mercy, a sinful sexual act, or other self-absorbed habits that diminish our moral fiber. By identifying moral dangers within our souls, we can better overcome them and heal from the wounds they cause. Welcoming discipline will humble our wills and help us cooperate with God's grace so as to bring about goodness and holiness within us.

We seek the formation of our wills as a training for virtue and as a nurturing of a desire for truth and goodness in our lives, as well as for peace within ourselves, with God, and with our neighbors. In summary, a properly formed will wants and pursues what is true, good, and beautiful in this life and prepares us for eternal fellowship with God in the next.

Reverence to Our Bodies and Those of Others

While many people today would attempt to solely define a "purity of heart" in terms of our bodies or sexual powers, we know that a pure heart involves many areas of our lives that call for generosity, love, and kindness. Nevertheless, while a pure heart is not exclusively about our sexual lives, it does involve them. And so, what does it mean to have a pure heart in terms of our sexuality?

In our world today, sexual expression is viewed in terms of gaining a supposed maturity, or as enjoyable leisure, or as some type of accomplishment. Love and responsibility as a part of our sexual expression are dismissed as restrictive, anti-quated, or unrealistic. People view sexual acts as a means of release or selfish gratification. Human dignity and personal worth are not a part of this contemporary game.

Our fallen world has forgotten the goodness and beauty of the human body. It neglects the importance of chastity and self-donation in the maturation of a person. Some people falsely believe that a loose expression of our sexual powers somehow bestows maturity or wisdom. In reality, such a loose moral life only causes a sense of meaninglessness. For us to grow in matu-rity and purity of heart, we must nurture a life of chastity, order our desires, and give ourselves as a sincere gift to others in vir-tue. Eventually, within the sacrament of Holy Matrimony, the sexual powers become a part of this self-donation.

Chastity, therefore, is about showing a reverence to our bodies and the bodies of others. It's about integrity. It's having control and harmony over our sexual desires and powers as a human person. It means we don't allow ourselves to live as ani-mals by raw instinct and passion. Chastity gives us the strength to be our true selves rather than the fragmented version that lust leaves in its wake. Chastity gives us freedom and prevents us from becoming slaves to our sexual passions, following them where they lead us and doing whatever they tell us.

Chastity also makes us honest. It won't tolerate double talk or duplicity. It's opposed to any behavior that is not ordered to truth and that would cause harm or impair our holistic well being.

The virtue of chastity is a personal task. It takes a particular form according to our state in life (married, single life, clergy, etc.). Chastity is a long and exacting work. And as we cooperate with God's grace and let chastity work, it molds and shapes us so that we can truly give ourselves to others.

Lazarus and the Lord's Purity of Heart

Throughout his public ministry, Jesus worked several signs and miracles to demonstrate the validity of his teachings. One of these last signs was the resurrection of his friend Lazarus.

While in another region, the apostles told Jesus of Lazarus's terminal illness. Jesus waited before going to Lazarus's home in Bethany, telling his disciples, "This illness is not unto death; it is for the glory of God, so that the Son of God may be glorified by means of it" (Jn 11:4).

The disciples did not understand what Jesus meant and were confused as to why the Lord would wait to go to his friend's home. In this interaction, Jesus reflected the purity of his heart as he saw the goodness and providence of God in the midst of human suffering and illness. The Lord's followers could not yet discern this goodness. There was a purity of heart, a trust and kindness, still lacking in their lives.

After his delay, Jesus finally went to see Lazarus. As he approached the home, Lazarus's sister Martha came out to greet him while Mary, the other sister, would not greet Jesus. Both siblings were distressed because their brother had died. They could not understand why Jesus would not have come earlier and healed him. As with the apostles, so with these two sisters; a purity of heart was not yet formed. They could not see a plan or goodness beyond their own hurt, sorrow, confusion, and grief. The two were not able to see God's providence or his loving kindness in the darkness.

In a conversation that reflects the custody of our minds and the formation of our wills, Jesus leads Martha into a deeper purity of heart. He calls her to open the eyes of her heart and see the Resurrection, the ultimate good of human life and history. Jesus invites her to a transcendence and beauty that can eclipse tragedy and disappointment, and allow her to see beyond herself:

> Martha said to Jesus, "Lord, if you had been here, my brother would not have died. And even now I know that whatever you ask from God, God will give you." Jesus said to her, "Your brother will rise again." Martha said to him, "I know that he will rise again in the resurrection at the last day." Jesus said to her, "I am the resurrection and the life; he who believes in me, though he die, yet shall he live, and whoever lives and believes in me shall never die. Do you believe this?" She said to him, "Yes, Lord; I believe that you are the Christ, the Son of God, he who is coming into the world." (Jn 11:21–27)

After Martha begins to see the power and glory of God, she is led to an act of charity. She goes to bring her sister to Jesus. As Jesus is molding their own hearts in purity and goodness, the Lord's own heart is moved with compassion. What follows is the shortest verse in the Bible, though it does not lack impact: "Jesus wept" (Jn 11:35). The Lord missed his friend and felt real, human sorrow. This demonstrates that a pure heart is not emotionless or stoical; in fact, a pure heart can feel emotions more deeply than an impure one, since there is nothing within it to pollute the emotions.

The Lord showed his pure, sacred heart and turned his emotions and attention to the greater good and to God's glory. Being led to where Lazarus was laid, Jesus turned to God the Father in prayer and commanded in a loud voice, "Lazarus, come out" (Jn 11:43). As we know the story goes, the dead man emerged from the cave wrapped in clothing and all were amazed.

The story of the resuscitation of Lazarus gives us an example of the pure heart of Jesus. It's a heart filled with love, trust, beauty, selfless service, openness, and conviction. This revelation stands as an example of our own summons to happiness and to a purity of heart that is available to us by God's grace.

Let us never forget that a pure heart is one that embraces and trusts in God's providence, knowing that he works "all things to the good of those who love him" (Rom 8:28), even if some of those things, like an earthly death, bring pain. A pure heart feels appropriate grief but does not grieve without hope because the pure in heart place great trust in God.

The Handmaid of the Lord

After the Lord Jesus himself, we can look to his first disciple, Mary of Nazareth. In Our Lady, we find the purest of hearts, shaped and designed by the perfection of God's grace, where all the attributes of a pure heart radiate throughout a difficult but happy life.

In many respects, Mary's purity of heart began at the very moment of her conception as she was conceived without sin, without any darkness or stain upon her soul. Then in her early life, she was taught to be a devout daughter of Israel and consecrated her life to God by a special vow of virginity.

When she reached the age for marriage, Joseph agreed to be her chaste spouse and to cherish and protect her. It was at this time that her struggles would intensify.

The angel Gabriel appeared to Our Lady and announced the incarnation of the Lord Jesus in her womb. Having a pure heart, Mary would honor her vow of virginity, and so questioned what was said to her: "How can this be, since I have no husband?" (Lk 1:34).

It should be noted that Mary was not doubting the power of God here. When Gabriel told Zachariah that his elderly wife, Elizabeth, would bear a child, he did doubt, and the angel struck him mute for his unbelief (see Lk 1:18–20). But here, Mary was not doubting, but literally asking how it would happen since she knew she had taken a vow of virginity.

Gabriel explained that the pregnancy would be by the power of the Most High and that the "Holy Spirit (would) come upon (her)." Mary, again showing the purity of her heart and her docility to God, responded, "Behold, I am the handmaid of the Lord; let it be to me according to your word" (Lk 1:38).

At this same moment, Our Lady was also told about the pregnancy of her older kinswoman. After the angel left, Mary went to Elizabeth in haste. This selfless and rapid charity further demonstrates Our Lady's purity of heart. Even after the appearance of an angel and the most important announcement ever given to humanity, Mary did not think of herself or her own situation but only of another person. This self-donation of time, energy, and affection are all indications of the beautiful purity of Our Lady's heart.

During the Lord's public ministry, Mary's purity of heart was particularly refined as it seemed there were times when he alienated himself from her and withheld natural affections. One time, in particular, Jesus was talking to a crowd while Mary stood outside with a few of his disciples. She wanted to speak to him, and someone informed Jesus that she was nearby. But Jesus replied, "Who is my mother, and who are my brethren?" Pointing to his disciples, he went on, "Here are my mother and my brethren! For whoever does the will of my Father in heaven is my brother, and sister, and mother" (Mt 12:48–50).

This must have been a shock to Our Lady, but Jesus was maturing her maternal affection and directing her to the vocation of First Disciple and Mother of humanity. In this gentle schooling, Jesus was preparing his mother for his future passion and his days in the tomb.

Our Lady's purity of heart was especially tested during her Son's passion and death. As she beheld her beloved son, her own flesh and blood, beaten, mocked, and tortured, she remained the *stabat mater*—the "standing mother"—broken of heart but bold in her rejection of the power of evil and despair. When everything seemed to break down and all hades appeared to break loose, Mary stood, without fear or question, declaring her hope in the goodness and the providence of God.

At Pentecost, when the Holy Spirit was sent after the ascension of the Lord Jesus, Mary was present with the apostles. Along with these early shepherds, she was also one of the first people to receive the Holy Spirit as tongues of fire. As the apostles were strengthened by the Holy Spirit for priestly ministry, Mary was emboldened by the Spirit for her vocation as Mother of the Church. Just as her pure heart served her divine Son, so that same immaculate and pure heart would serve his disciples.

At the end of the earthly life, Mary was assumed body and soul into eternity. The Lord could not allow any decay or corruption to touch the body of his mother. In this divine act of love, the eternal reward and the glory of those who fight to preserve a pure heart is displayed; namely, that the pure of heart will see God and have fellowship with him.

"And Now I See . . ."

On one occasion in the Lord's public ministry, he was asked by his disciples about a blind man. They wanted to know whether the man was blind because of his sins or the sins of his parents. The Lord indicated that neither were at fault but that the man was blind in order to show the glory of God.

After indicating that he was doing the work of the Father, Jesus spit on the ground, made some mud, and put it on the man's eyes. He then told the man to go and wash in the Pool of Siloam. As the man did so, he was restored to sight, announcing, "Though I was blind, now I see" (Jn 9:25).

This man was scrutinized and mistreated because of his cure, as many doubted him and wrote him off as a fool. Nonetheless, he stands as a reminder and example of what it means to seek a pure heart. The man was open to the Lord's help, he was willing to accept saliva-mud on his eyes, and he went to the Pool of Siloam as he was told, and he was healed and able to see. In response to the miracle, the Pharisees were defiant and refused to see, and so the Lord taught, "For judgment I came into this world, that those who do not see may see, and those that see may become blind" (Jn 9:39).

How will we respond to the Lord's initiative in our lives? Will we be receptive to God's help? Are we willing to get our hands and eyes dirty so that we can realize the good things of the earth and the providence of God? And are we willing to cooperate and do what God asks of us to be healed so that we can also see?

The Lord uses our created world to minister to us. He made it good and we must acknowledge this beauty and respect it. We must see God's vestige in our world, in created things, and in our bodies. We also have to be active in the work to purify our hearts. We have to seek out the sacraments, especially Holy Communion and confession. We need to read the Sacred Scriptures, pray, seek holy fellowship, and generously serve those in need. In these ways, like washing in the Pool of Siloam, we allow God to absolve our sins, remove hurtful things from our souls, restore our bodies to goodness, open our eyes to see him, and lead us along the sure path of happiness and holiness.

Seeking a pure heart is to desire faithfulness in our lives, with our feelings, thoughts, words, and actions. It shows a trust in God, a docility to goodness, a love for neighbor, and a chastity of mind and body.

Lust is the opposite. It's the anti-beatitude. It craves for pleasure in a disordered and immoral way. It longs for euphoria, highs, and self-indulgence. Lust cares for nothing other than its own pursuit of gratification and appeasement. When entertained, lust consumes the person. Other people become mere objects of pleasure or utility. The ability to experience transcendence or see the providence of God becomes blurred and shady.

And so our decision is either for happiness and the transparency of life given by a pure heart or misery and the self-absorbed world of lust and momentary pleasures. One path provides freedom, love, and virtue, while the other is bloated within itself, enslaved to ego, and consumed by an enticement to vice.

The choice is ours. How will we choose to live?

Mount to Mission

Purity of heart is difficult to attain and preserve, especially in a secularized and promiscuous culture, but it is not impossible. For us to allow grace to form a pure heart within us, we have to grow in faith and confidence. We must forgive and embrace those in need. We must desire and accept the will of God and not the will of our earthly pleasures. We must die to ourselves in order to understand and minister to others and their needs. Rather than absorbing our hearts with a fallen love for material things, emotional indulgence, or physical pleasure, we should use our minds and bodies, and the things of this world, in a tempered and ordered way, while also being attentive to the needs of our neighbors.

We must purify our intentions, making them transparent. We should avoid duplicity and focus our imaginations and memories to virtue. We need to avoid outbursts, or disrespect, or rash judgment of others and seek a reasonable response to all and a tempering of virtue that leads us to innocence and a deference to God and others.

In describing the challenges of living with a pure heart, it might help us to assess different situations in which such purity is tested:

- The poor man who finds money on the ground and wants to keep it but gives it to the rightful owner, even though he could use it for his own needs.

- The married man who is tempted to objectify his wife but fights against it and nurtures affection and respect toward her.

- The woman who, in the midst of her own responsibilities, sees an elderly man in need and escorts him across the road, even though it will make her late to her next appointment.

- The married woman whose husband is seriously ill and doesn't understand why God won't grant a healing, and yet praises God and seeks to see his providence in the midst of the suffering.

- A young man who realizes he's becoming addicted to pornography goes to his father and humbles himself by asking for help to break the habit.

In all these cases and more, a pure heart leads us to virtuous actions, which in turn leads us to happiness.

Examination of Conscience

- Do I trust in God's providence and seek his goodness in my life, especially in dark or difficult times?

- Do I perform good deeds for God or because of the opinions of others?

- Are my imagination, memories, and thoughts wholesome and conforming to virtue?

- Do I ignore or make excuses for my faults and sins?

- Do I objectify the bodies of others?

- Am I a forgiving person, seeing another's goodness beyond their faults and offenses?

- Do I seek recognition for my good deeds?

- Do I look for opportunities to strengthen my will by acts of penance or mortification?

- Am I an understanding person, trying to listen and show empathy to the struggles or situations of others?

- Do I receive the sacraments regularly and look for other ways to grow in the spiritual life?

School of Discipleship

Continuing in our School of Discipleship, it is now time to look at the sixth beatitude: **pure of heart.**

As we try to nurture a pure heart, the Holy Spirit bestows us with the gift of **understanding**. When we understand something we have transparency, meaning it is clear to us. As the promise of this beatitude states, the pure of heart will see God, meaning they will have complete clarity concerning his will for their lives and for the world.

Once we receive this gift, the virtue of **faith** is perfected in our soul. The *Catechism* says faith is "the virtue by which we believe in God and believe all that he has said and revealed to us. . . . For this reason the believer seeks to know and do God's will" (CCC 1814). In gaining clarity for God's will, our faith is strengthened because we see his plan and purpose for our lives, and those with a strong faith are the ones who will see God.

This beatitude, gift, and virtue help us to better understand the petition in the Lord's Prayer **"And lead us not into temptation,"** as faith and understanding help us to see the scope of evil, the intentions of the wicked, and the occasions of sin. When received and exercised well, they can help us persevere in our struggle to obtain a pure heart. The blossoming of this petition is the promise of this beatitude, which is to see God. If we are led "not into temptation," then we are led instead to God.

Lastly, the path that begins from this beatitude and crosses through these other aspects of the spiritual life help us to recognize the foul and self-centered nature of the capital sin of **lust**. It should not surprise us that this is the anti-beatitude of those with a pure heart. The person enslaved to lust is absorbed in himself and cannot understand the needs or dignity of others. He has no clarity concerning God's will because he is blinded by his passions, and his faith is weakened by his sins.

Seeking a pure heart is to desire faithfulness in our lives, with our feelings, thoughts, words, and actions. It shows a trust in God, a docility to goodness, a love for neighbor, and a chastity of mind and body.

Lust is the opposite. It craves for pleasure in a disordered and immoral way. It longs for euphoria, highs, and self-indulgence. Lust cares for nothing other than its own pursuit of gratification and appeasement. When entertained, lust consumes the person. Other people become mere objects of pleasure or utility. The ability to experience transcendence or see the providence of God becomes blurred and shady.

As the promise of a pure heart is to see God, so the punishment of the anti-beatitude is to be blinded by our passions and be led into temptation and away from God.

BEATITUDE	GIFT OF THE SPIRIT	CORRESPONDING VIRTUE	PETITION OF THE LORD'S PRAYER	CAPITAL SIN/ ANTI-BEATITUDE
Blessed are the pure in heart, for they shall see God	Understanding	Faith	And lead us not into temptation	Lust

Prayer

All-Present and Loving Father,
Give me a pure heart to see you.
Keep lust away from my heart. Teach me generosity and gentleness.
Help me to see the needs of others.
Never let me indulge in darkness or become enslaved to sexual sin.
Come to me, Father, and bless me with greater faith and temperance.
Bring me into your kingdom! Show me happiness.
Through Christ our Lord. Amen.

Three Helpful Truths to Have a Pure Heart:

+ God is all-holy and the source of all purity.
+ I am called to have a pure heart, which is living chastely, kindly, and selflessly toward others.
+ I do not have the strength to keep a pure heart, and so I need to use the means of holiness given to me, especially the sacraments, to persevere and grow in a purity of heart.

The Prayer of the Lord Jesus

I do not pray that you should take them out of the world, but that you should keep them from the evil one. They are not of the world, even as I am not of the world. Sanctify them in the truth; your word is truth. As you sent me into the world, so I have sent them into the world. And for their sake I consecrate myself, that they also may be consecrated in truth.

John 17:15–19

The Psalmist's Petition

Create in me a clean heart, O God,
And put a new and right spirit within me.
Cast me not away from your presence,
and take not your holy Spirit from me.
Restore to me the joy of your salvation,
and uphold me with a willing spirit.

Psalm 51:10–12

CHAPTER 7

The Peacemakers

*Blessed are the peacemakers, for they
shall be called sons of God.*

MATTHEW 5:9

Operation New Horizons

When I was a college student at the Franciscan University of Steubenville, I enlisted in the Army National Guard. I come from a long family of Army veterans, so serving in the military was an unspoken expectation. I was happy to serve and was greatly helped by the monetary assistance toward my education. My enlistment predated the attacks on the World Trade Center in 2001; this meant there was no serious sense that National Guardsmen, who at that time were principally committed to the service of a specific state, would be activated for a foreign mission.

At least, that was the presumption until Hurricane Mitch hit Central America in late fall of 1998. It was the second deadliest Atlantic hurricane on record, leading to massive loss of life and destruction of property. In particular, the entire infrastructure of several countries—roads, bridges, railways, hospitals, market places, and schools—was completely gone. Reconstruction and relief efforts needed extensive international assistance.

The United States stepped up and commissioned "Operation New Horizons," a military-led humanitarian task force with the responsibility of rebuilding necessary public resources in several Central American countries, such as Honduras, Guatemala, and Nicaragua. And so I received my activation orders and was sent to the region of Esteli in western Nicaragua. While there, I helped to clear vast debris and rebuild a road that would allow local people to walk to the river for water. We also began to rebuild a school and medical clinic. In Esteli alone, there were thousands of American soldiers doing similar work. All of us were in uniform, under military commands, and protected by necessary weaponry and armaments from rebel guerillas who roamed that area of the country.

It might strike some as an odd parallel: soldiers working within a system designed to prepare them for war now actively engaged in humanitarian relief efforts. But are the two scenarios truly at odds? What does the Lord's assured blessing to peacemakers really look like?

Oftentimes the depth and richness of peace is diminished in contemporary use. It becomes merely synonymous with pacifism, which is an absence of war, conflict, or tension. While these are certainly favored results of peace, they are not by themselves a complete or substantial definition of peace.

Biblically understood, peace begins with an acknowledgment of the Creator, of human dignity, and of the knowledge of right from wrong. From this series of recognitions, peace is a tranquility of order. We achieve peace when we know and accept our vocation and perform it virtuously and well, when we respect the dignity and roles of others, and when we all mutually seek the common good together for the flourishing of the human person and the building up of society and culture.

Even beyond Scripture, we see this understanding of peace in the founding of the United States: "We hold these truths to be self-evident: that all men are created equal; that they are endowed by their Creator with certain unalienable rights; that among these are life, liberty, and the pursuit of happiness."

It was precisely the violation of order, such as over taxation and the abuse of human rights, by the British monarch that broke the peace, leading to the revolution and the American Revolutionary War. The war itself did not break the peace, but the abuses leading up to it, which introduced disharmony into the relationship between two nations. In fact, the war's purpose was to reestablish order and thereby reestablish peace. While conflict can be used for evil, it becomes a source of order and the preservation of goodness when it is in service to peace. Traditionally, this type of conflict is known as a just war.

In comprehending what peace is, it should not strike the observer as odd that soldiers are doing humanitarian work since their very purpose is to preserve peace and protect the common good. Soldiers from just and well-meaning nations are not thugs or barbarians. They are willing to fight and die for peace, just as they are willing to rebuild roads and hospitals for the sake of peace. Either type of service facilitates and defends the tranquility of order in one way or another.

This brings us back to the Lord's promise in Matthew 5:9. Peacemakers are not superficial people who violate or overlook the common good solely to avoid conflict or tension. This is not peace but appeasement. Appeasement may give a temporary consolation that resembles peace, but the offense that necessitated the appeasement will continue to fester and linger, often coming back to harm the common good even more than it would have to begin with had the appeasement not been sought.

Peace has never been won by the fainthearted. Scripture makes it clear how much God detests cowardice, comparing the cowardly to murderers, fornicators, and idolaters who will one day be thrown into "the lake that burns with fire and brimstone" (Rv 21:8). Rather, the ones who foster peace are those who have the courage to take a stand for what is right, and those who submit to God and his will. Peacemakers cherish human dignity and the common good, know human rights and human responsibilities, and can distinguish right from wrong based on the tranquility of order. They speak the truth even when inconvenient, and are bold and selfless in their service and defense of goodness.

These are the ones who will be called the children of God. Will we make peace or accept appeasement? Will we choose this sure but difficult path to happiness?

Peace—A Divine Gift

The very first words of the Bible read as follows: "In the beginning God created the heavens and the earth. The earth was without form and void, and darkness was upon the face of the deep; and the Spirit of God was moving over the face of the waters. And God said, 'Let there be light'; and there was light" (Gn 1:1–3).

This biblical imagery expresses the truth that God created all things and then brought them into form, giving them an order and structure. God then created man and woman in his own image and placed them as stewards of the earth and this order within it. When this order is respected and fulfilled, when it is being lived out well, there is tranquility among all things. This tranquility is like a song. If the written music, the various instruments, and the musicians themselves all work together under the direction of a conductor, then a beautiful piece of music is performed.

Peace, therefore, is bestowed upon us as a divine gift. It's a sign of God's favor to us and of his presence among us.

If only the Genesis account of creation could stop there. But there's more, and sadly it gets darker. At this point, the Book of Genesis uses "figurative language" (see CCC 390). It describes a garden that our first parents were to care for and use as a place to start a family.

In the garden was also the Tree of the Knowledge of Good and Evil, and God told his beloved children not to eat from that tree (see Gn 2:16–17). The tree was not merely a source of cognitive knowledge of right from wrong, but rather the actual power *to determine* what is good and what is evil. This is what philosophy calls relativism, which is when a person believes that he is the measure of reality, the center of the universe, and can by his own will determine whether something is right or wrong.

The command not to eat from such a tree, therefore, was not some type of distorted power play on God's part, or some attempt to exclude Adam and Eve from some type of necessary ability or food. The command was born from God's loving kindness; the same kindness that created and sustained our first parents. God told them not to eat of the Tree of the Knowledge of Good and Evil because human nature does not have the capacity to use or control such ability. The task of determining right and wrong requires the ability to see all things and to intimately know all things, vision or knowledge that we sorely lack. They are "super" (which means "above") our nature; thus, they are supernatural. It would have been cruel for God to give us the power to determine good and evil.

An example might help. What if I was to go to a local stable, approach a horse, and ask it to tell me what two plus two equals? Of course the horse wouldn't answer me. Imagine if I asked again in a louder voice, and even began to punch and harass the horse demanding that it tell me what two plus two equals. What would you think?

Admittedly, someone observing this exchange could rightly accuse me of animal cruelty. "Leave the horse alone," they might yell at me. My interaction with the horse would be malicious since a horse has a proper horse nature incapable of doing mathematics and unable to express itself through verbal communication. It would be wrong to expect abilities from a created thing that does not have the capacity to fulfill those expectations. We can't expect the spoken answer of four from a horse!

In a similar manner, God told our first parents to avoid relativism since human nature does not have the capacity to fulfill the demands of giving moral identity to an action (to decide whether something is good or evil). We don't have the proper nature for such actions. As contemporary business language would say, "It's above our skill set!"

But as we know the story goes, Adam and Eve disobeyed

and sought to have a majesty above their natural state. God's love is displayed in the aftermath of this disobedience, as he did not come in vengeance or rage to find our first parents. Instead, God searched them out and desired to walk with them "in the garden in the cool of the day" (Gn 3:8). When he couldn't see them, he asked, "Where are you?" (Gn 3:9).

Adam responded, "I heard the sound of you in the garden, and I was afraid, because I was naked; and I hid myself." So God asked him, "Who told you that you were naked?" (Gn 3:10–11).

God has now asked two questions, but of course he already knew the answers. God never asks a question to discover an answer; he has all the answers! He was simply showing his paternal kindness as he knew of his children's guilt and attempted to provide them with an opportunity to confess their disobedience. But rather than repent, Adam and Eve both played a blame game and refused to accept their fault; Adam blamed Eve, and Eve the serpent.

The Disorder of Sin

The original sin of our first parents caused humanity's and all creation's fall from grace. It introduced a break in the peace and harmony between God and humanity, within our own bodies and souls, within our fellowship with others, and between humanity and the whole of creation.

On account of the Fall, we now fear God as a human family. We invent caricatures of him that falsely show him as angry and seeking vengeance. Rather than seeing him as a loving Father, we turn him into a distant tyrant or a wrathful judge.

Original sin also weakens and wounds our human nature. Our intellects are now clouded, our wills are frail, our memories and imaginations are inconsistent, and our emotions are impulsive. Overall, our souls are now fragile and our bodies corruptible. Our inner peace is disturbed and we find a battle within ourselves for goodness. We are shocked by our attraction or inclination to darkness, even when we know it is wrong and harmful to us and our true happiness.

Original sin also severed peace in terms of our relationship with our neighbors. In particular, a tension is introduced among spouses in marriage. Nuptial union is supposed to be a place of love, self-donation, and selfless service, but it can now become the seedbed of resentment, anger, and bitterness. Spouses, who are called to reflect the friendship between God and humanity, can quickly become tired and vicious to one another because of selfishness, greed, and a will to power. As this discord can be found in marriages, so it can spread to families, neighborhoods, work places, circles of friends, and society as a whole. This can escalate and be found even among whole peoples or nations. This lack of peace is summarized by the Catholic philosopher Blaise Pascal, who famously said, "Wars happen because men cannot sit quietly in their own rooms."

A breach of harmony is also found in the human family's relationship with creation. We approach the world as its master rather than its steward. We can forget our vocation to care for our environment and give attention to our common home. Rather than approaching it with prudence and temperance, we can cause it harm for reasons of profit, domination, irresponsibility, or misplaced leisure.

All of the above, caused by sin, breaks peace and permits

chaos. Examining the word *sin* might further help us to understand its consequences. The term is actually from the Hebrew word *chata*, which means "to miss" or "to go wrong." It's actually a sports term from archery that was first used in reference to slingers of stone, especially the left-handed slingers from the Tribe of Benjamin in the Old Testament (cf. Jgs 20:16; 1 Chr 12:2). If a slinger or an archer threw a stone or shot an arrow and missed his target, then he "sinned." It was incomplete, not on the spot, and left something lacking. It was something that called the athlete to greater practice and discipline so that he wouldn't "sin" in the future.

This context is helpful to us. In life, sin as a moral fault has a similar meaning. When we sin, we miss the mark. Peace is disturbed, and rather than a tranquility of order, disorder is brought into our lives and the world. The sports imagery should be encouraging to us since sin does not destroy or abolish order; it simply fails to hit the target spot on. For sin to be removed and peace restored, we have to accept God's grace and labor for virtue and goodness.

Hopefully now we understand that peace is a divine gift, but it is a gift threatened by the disorder of sin. For peace to be received and lived, it requires discipline, selflessness, and cooperation with grace. By ourselves, we cannot secure peace, but luckily, God realized this and did something about it. He came to us as the Prince of Peace.

The Prince of Peace

The Lord Jesus was hailed by the prophet Isaiah as "the Prince of Peace," and by his cross and resurrection, he destroyed sin, healed its disorder, reestablished tranquility, secured our freedom, and offered peace to the children of God (cf. Is 9:6; Jn 20:21; Gal 5:1).

What exactly does this mean? If we return to our previous example of a piece of music, we see how important it is for every part to be accurate and excellent for beautiful music to be performed. In particular, the conductor has to know the music, the instruments, and his musicians. But what could a good conductor do if there's a mistake? A conductor could stop the entire piece and conclude the performance: "That's it! It's ruined!" Or he could pretend he didn't hear the error and act as if nothing happened: "What? What mistake? I didn't notice!" Or if the conductor wants a well-ordered piece, he could use the mistake as the first note of a new, spontaneous—yet ordered—sequence in the music. This would require a holistic understanding of the piece and an extreme ability to write while also conducting. It's also necessary that the musicians "play along" and cooperate with the conductor in this new work.

This scenario with the conductor can be applied to our own world. A mistake was introduced to the musical score of humanity through Adam and Eve's disobedience. Their sin broke the harmony (the peace) that God intended for us to have within ourselves, with each other, with creation, and with him.

But being an all-knowing, all-loving, and all-powerful "conductor," he sought to give us a new beginning. He took our mistake and created a new sequence of music that began with a young virgin in Nazareth.

When the time came, the archangel Gabriel appeared to Mary to announce the conception of the Son of God, saying, "The Holy Spirit will come upon you, and the power of the

Most High will overshadow you" (Lk 1:35). Recall the imagery from Genesis, when the Spirit of God "hovered over" the formless, empty, and dark waters at the beginning of time. There was peace and order in this creation narrative until our first parents broke it. Now the Spirit hovers over Our Lady as her divine Son, Jesus Christ, will come to restore this lost peace and begin the work of redemption for all time.

And so the eternal Son of God came to us. He lived a fully human life, and by his passion, death, and resurrection, he brought about reconciliation and restored peace between our fallen race and God the Father. As the Lord Jesus prepared for his passion, he told us, "Peace I leave with you; my peace I give to you; not as the world gives do I give to you. Let not your hearts be troubled, neither let them be afraid" (Jn 14:27).

In this teaching, Jesus is distinguishing true peace from the peace of this world. The peace offered by the Lord is a tranquility of order that requires truth, strong virtue, and a love of goodness. The peace of this world is a false peace based on appeasement, compromise, and a "culture of nice" where everything and anything is acceptable. In such an enclosed world, reality is eclipsed and words such as *tolerance* are redefined and misunderstood. Disorder of sin is then normalized, and we begin to accept evil, or even champion it. Key human concepts like love, freedom, and mercy are defined to mean whatever anyone wants them to mean. The Lord breaks through this worldly peace and tells us clearly:

> Do not think that I have come to bring peace on earth; I have not come to bring peace, but a sword. For I have come to set a man against his father, and a daughter against her mother, and a daughter-in-law against her mother-in-law; and a man's foes will be

those of his own household. He who loves father or mother more than me is not worthy of me; and he who loves son or daughter more than me is not worthy of me; and he who does not take his cross and follow me is not worthy of me. He who finds his life will lose it, and he who loses his life for my sake will find it. (Mt 10:34–39)

This peace he is referring to, the kind he did *not* come to bring us, refers to the false peace of the world. He did not come here to ensure that everyone be nice to each other at the expense of overlooking sin. The peace he does want to bring us takes effort, fortitude, and selflessness. It requires a singular devotion to Jesus Christ and a willingness to pick up our own cross. He brought peace to the world by carrying his; now we must follow his example and pick up ours if we wish to obtain peace of soul.

In the person of Jesus Christ, therefore, we see a restoration and a new beginning of peace for the human family, a tranquility of order between God and humanity, within the human heart, among neighbors, and between humanity and the rest of creation. In Jesus Christ, the God-Man, we are blessed with this peace. It is a peace that requires our cooperation with grace, which is the life of God within us, and so for those who seek and are willing to fight for peace, they become the children of God.

Will we be peacemakers? Will we accept the happiness that comes from true peace?

Jesus, Martha, and Mary

On one occasion in his public ministry, Jesus went to the home of two sisters, Martha and Mary. We can imagine that he was tired from his work and travels and was seeking retreat in the home of these two sisters.

When he arrived, Martha was very busy making arrangements for his stay. She was a busy-body, the type of hostess who serves but lacks a certain kind of grace since her service precludes her actually sitting down and visiting with her guest. Mary, meanwhile, chose to spend her time not in domestic preparation but sitting at the Lord's feet and listening to his teachings (see Lk 10:39).

Eventually, Martha becomes very frustrated and asks Jesus, "Lord, do you not care that my sister has left me to serve alone? Tell her then to help me" (Lk 10:40). Obviously, peace is lacking between the two sisters, and as far as Martha is concerned, it's because of Mary. But Jesus turns the focus back to Martha as the source of their sisterly disharmony. "Martha, Martha, you are anxious and troubled about many things; one thing is needful. Mary has chosen the good portion, which shall not be taken away from her" (vv. 41–42).

In this conversation, we see Jesus as a peacemaker on a "micro level," here in the home of two sisters, in the hustle and bustle of housework. This should remind us that while world peace is important, we need to look for opportunities in our daily lives to establish, nurture, and defend peace. Most people will not need to look beyond their own marriages, families, or work places to find such occasions to be peacemakers.

The Lord reminds Martha of how important communion with God is. Such things as hospitality and providing earthly comforts to others, while important, pale in comparison to us bringing God into our lives (and bringing God to others). Prepared meals and clean bathrooms will pass with time, but love, sincerely exchanged, is eternal. The Lord, therefore, points the way back to peace and invites Martha to take the journey.

In our own lives, the Lord calls us to appreciate the here and now. He leads us to prayer and communion with him and calls us to hospitality of the heart. In pursuing these well, we nurture peace and experience the happiness that comes from it.

The Conversion of Zacchaeus

In the course of his travels, Jesus passed through Jericho. A chief tax collector there named Zacchaeus had heard about Jesus and wanted to see him. But there was just one problem; Zacchaeus was short and couldn't see over the crowd. Eventually, he ran ahead and climbed a sycamore tree so that he could see Jesus.

When the Lord passed under this tree, he looked up and said, "Zacchaeus, make haste and come down; for I must stay at your house today" (Lk 19:5). The tax collector quickly came down and greeted Jesus joyfully.

Since many people heard this conversation, they began to murmur, "He has gone in to be the guest of a man who is a sinner" (Lk 19:7). It's well known that tax collectors were the bane of society, men who often cheated their own people. Zacchaeus was presumably guilty of many crimes. Nonetheless, he stood up and made it a point to amend his ways, saying, "Behold, Lord, the half of my goods I give to the poor; and if I have defrauded any one of anything, I restore it four-fold" (v. 8). Jesus replied, "Today salvation has come to this house, since he also is a son of Abraham. For the Son of man came to seek and save the lost" (vv. 9–10).

This conversion is a telling one since Zacchaeus realized that, as he encountered the Lord and desired to follow him, he needed to restore peace. The kindness of the Lord and the forgiveness of Zacchaeus's sins led the former chief tax collector to an awareness of the harm he had caused others and the imposition he placed on their well-being. The resolutions he made to the Lord—to give half his possessions to the poor and four times repayment to anyone he cheated—are acts of a peacemaker. These were acts of penance that reestablished peace between Zacchaeus and God, within the man's soul itself, and among his neighbors.

In our own lives, when we perform penance after making a heartfelt confession, the same peace that came to Zacchaeus comes unto us. The Lord accepted his resolutions, declared him a son of Abraham, and assured him salvation; and so he will do for us if we also repent. This is the reward of repentance: to become a son of Abraham, a child of God, and to have the peace and happiness of salvation bestowed upon us.

Will we follow the selfless but rewarding path of Zacchaeus? Will we be peacemakers and cherish the happiness that comes from it?

The Barnabas Principle

In the early Church, there were many growing pains. The life of Saul of Tarsus displays this. He had been a persecutor of Christians and after his conversion, many believers still did not trust him, and some were outright afraid of him.

When Saul, who then became Paul after his conversion, returned to Jerusalem, Barnabas rallied his cause and persuaded the apostles to let the former persecutor have fellowship with them (see Acts 9:26). As a result, a close friendship developed between the two and both were sent on a mission together.

On Paul and Barnabas's first missionary journey, Barnabas brought his younger cousin, John Mark (Col 4:10). The young man's parents were early disciples of the Lord, and he may have met Jesus as a boy (Acts 12:12; Mk 14:51–52). Now, as a young adult, he wanted to be involved in the apostolic work of the Church. Incidentally, later in John Mark's life, he became a disciple of St. Peter in Rome and wrote the Gospel book that bears his name (cf. 1 Pt 5:13).

Along the way of this first missionary effort, however, John Mark grew faint-hearted and decided to return to Jerusalem (Acts 13:13). It's generally believed that he was too young and was overwhelmed by the campaign.

Later on, when Paul and Barnabas planned a second journey, Barnabas wanted to take John Mark, but Paul refused. The Acts of the Apostles indicate that a "sharp contention" grew between them (Acts 15:36–41). The two apostles could not reach a settlement, and so the two peacefully went separate ways. It is most likely that Paul and Barnabas never saw each other again in this life. Each apostle, however, continued to do outstanding work for God's kingdom and actively spread the Gospel. In the end, both died martyrs for the Faith.

This biblical account gives rise to what is oftentimes called the "Barnabas Principle," which is applied when two virtuous people are called to do a good work separately. In the false peace of this world, any disagreement, separation, tension, or authentic diversity is denounced. Everyone must "get along" in the exact same way. Even as certain ideologies cry for tolerance, it's disturbing how intolerant such views are toward those who do not agree with them.

As certain schools of thought and social activism discard the very "order" that gives peace its substance, so they impose, far more viciously than any true peacemaker would, a new self-engineered order where superficial things and sincere disagreements are seen as an unacceptable dissent, a dangerous deviation, and something that needs to be shamed or ostracized as soon as possible.

In the Barnabas Principle, conversely, disputes and differences are discerned and welcomed when they serve and expand the common good. With an objective order guiding peace, there is space and openness for a diversity of temperaments, courses of action, and ways of explaining or expressing the things of life. Truth be told, no fallen person appreciates being disagreed with, as we can imagine St. Paul didn't like St. Barnabas's difference of opinion. And yet, when there is an ordered peace, personality or emotions are not permitted to have the last word and instead are humbled by the tranquility of order.

A properly understood peace is able to absorb tension, realizing that it can initiate better, greater, or more expansive service to the common good. On such occasions, peace is not restricted to a mere absence of tension or conflict. Quite the opposite, peace can facilitate and guide conflict so that its energies can serve the good of society and not the pride of any one person.

The Barnabas Principle—and its clarification of peace—can be summarized well by the maxim of Pope St. John XXIII who famously taught:

In essentials, unity;
In non-essentials, diversity;
In all things, charity.

Mount to Mission

The main goal of our lives is to seek the peace of God. Divine Providence bestows this peace and gives it an order or structure, expressed in both revelation and through human reason. We can see this providential order in the Christian tradition, the Bible, the teachings of the Church, and the natural moral law, which is written on our hearts as human beings. In these different ways, we can discern this order and discover what we are called to be and do in this life. As we conform to this summons, we will find peace. Even if trying to live by this order causes us internal tension, we understand that this is a beneficial suffering since a greater good is being brought forth in us. If our desire to follow an ordered peace brings disagreement, we will stay the course knowing that peace is found in truth and goodness and not in compromise or empty civility.

As Christians, therefore, we must implement peace in all that we say and do. We must labor to pray devoutly, serve society, accompany the forgotten, advocate for the victimized, console friends, encourage neighbors, teach children, defend virtue, comfort the sick and suffering, cherish marriage and family, and otherwise seek active ways in which to express the peace of God in our world today.

Pope St. John Paul II said on many occasions that "we are most like God when we bring order from chaos." This is the task of the peacemaker. The person committed to peace will speak up and act when he should; he will not allow evil to go unchallenged or good to go unsupported. He sees what must be done and does his best to bring about a tranquility of order. In these ways, the peacemaker is a child of God as he lives by God's providential order and reflects in his words and actions the peace that is being brought about by Jesus Christ, the eternal Son of God.

When present, the tranquility of order is reflected by the fruits of God's Spirit: charity, joy, peace, patience, kindness, goodness, generosity, gentleness, faithfulness, modesty, self-control, and chastity (cf. Is 32:15–18; Gal 5:22–23).

The path of happiness and the work of peace are also described by the corporal and spiritual works of mercy:

CORPORAL WORKS OF MERCY	SPIRITUAL WORKS OF MERCY
To feed the hungry.	To instruct the uneducated.
To give drink to the thirsty.	To counsel the doubtful.
To clothed the naked.	To admonish the sinners.
To shelter the homeless.	To bear patiently those who wrong us.
To visit the sick.	To forgive offenses.
To visit the imprisoned.	To comfort the afflicted.
To bury the dead.	To pray for the living and the dead.

If we perform all these works of mercy, not only do we bring comfort and solace to our neighbor, but we open ourselves up to the peace of God.

Here are some practical, "in the trenches" situations of people trying to be peacemakers in their lives today:

- The woman who mediates an argument between coworkers even though they are both rude to her.

- The teenager who stands up for others who are being bullied at school running the risk of being bullied himself.

- The divorced parent who stays active in the life and moral formation of his children even though such involvement causes tension with his former spouse.

- The person with same-sex attraction who heroically orders his desires according to truth and goodness.

- The young adult who prays in front of an abortion clinic every weekend, sacrificing other activities with friends.

- The police officer who treats criminal offenders with respect even when they mock or oppose his attempts to serve and protect.

The peace that comes from right choices being made in all these situations, and many more, ultimately leads us to happiness.

Examination of Conscience

- Do I pray and seek to know God's providential order in my life?

- Do I stand up for those who cannot stand up for themselves?

- Do I actively seek ways to virtuously fulfill the duties of my state in life?

- Am I a coward or influenced by vanity or human respect in standing up for moral goodness or for those in need?

- Do I settle for the peace of this world with its compromise and false civility?

- Do I seek to order my affections, desires, and passions according to the standards of true peace and moral goodness?

- Am I easily offended by disagreements or differences of opinion?

- Do I look for opportunities to reconcile people who have a strained relationship?

- Do I consider the poor and those in need while managing my time and finances?

- Do I look for opportunities to live the works of mercy in my life and in the lives of those under my care?

School of Discipleship

Continuing in our School of Discipleship, it is now time to look at the seventh beatitude: **the peacemakers.**

If we strive to become a peacemaker, the Holy Spirit will bestow upon us the gift of **wisdom**. A wise person understands God's providence. Wisdom helps him see earthly things in light of eternity, and in doing so, he nourishes a detachment from those earthly things. The wise man does not value what only profits him corporally; conversely, he values greatly the things that will get him to heaven, chiefly peace of soul. The wise man is at peace because of the knowledge he has of what really matters in life, and by extension, he spreads that peace to those around him. This is why so many wise men carry themselves with calm and peace.

Once we receive this gift, the virtue of **charity** is perfected in our soul, which is another word for love. The *Catechism* says charity is "the virtue by which we love God above all things for his own sake, and our neighbor as ourselves for the love of God" (CCC 1822). As we seek to know the hearts of God and of our neighbors through wisdom, we are brought into a broader horizon that allows us to live a more generous life of love and charity.

This beatitude, gift, and virtue help us to understand the petition in the Lord's Prayer **"But deliver us from evil"** since wisdom and charity help us to trust God, perceive his providential order, discern its guidance in our lives, and boldly follow him. The blossoming of this petition is the promise of this beatitude, that we will be called children of God. If we are delivered from evil, delivered from being children of the evil one, then we will instead be children of God.

Lastly, the path that begins from this beatitude and crosses through these other aspects of the spiritual life helps us identify the tragedy and self-centeredness of the capital sin of **gluttony**. The life of a glutton is focused on himself and has very little room for anyone or for any other good thing. A glutton seeks to block peace since he obsesses, overindulges, and exaggerates one part of creation's order. Peace is marked by a sense of balance and harmony, whereas gluttony is identified by extremism and polarity.

The person bloated by gluttony cannot understand the needs or love of others. Such a person is stuck in a cesspool of their own passions and desires. He loves himself too much, taking in everything for himself, forfeiting a love of neighbor and a life of self-donation. The glutton consumes the world, the peacemaker pours out himself into the world to make it a better (a more peaceful and ordered) place.

A glutton does not just pursue money, power, food, drink, or pleasure to satisfy a need or a legitimate want, but will actually pursue these created goods beyond what is necessary or even healthy. His wants have no end. The glutton thinks only of himself. He does not care about the one who suffers because of his own craving for consolation. He does not want the poor to have food because he desires food only for himself and his enjoyment. The glutton does not want a sinner to undergo conversion because he wants the person to sin for him or his pleasure. The glutton cannot care about the things of God because he is only focused on his own divinization by usurping a height, fulfillment, or glory that properly belongs only to God.

The peacemaker forgives and works to conclude arguments, tension, or strife through truth, love, and selfless service. The glutton, however, feeds animosity and friction by selfishly demanding and insisting on his own favor, goals, rights, or desires.

A peacemaker sees the whole order of creation and is selfless. He is willing to sacrifice for the sake of others and the common good. By contrast, a glutton sacrifices the good of others to enhance his own prosperity.

As the promise of being a peacemaker is to be called children of God, so the punishment of the anti-beatitude is to only be a child of himself (and thus, the evil one) since he displays the ongoing self-centeredness and immaturity of a juvenile who never grows up and who never sees the greater world around him.

In conclusion, the seventh row of our spiritual matrix looks like this:

BEATITUDE	GIFT OF THE SPIRIT	CORRESPONDING VIRTUE	PETITION OF THE LORD'S PRAYER	CAPITAL SIN/ ANTI-BEATITUDE
Blessed are the peace-makers, for they shall be called sons of God	Wisdom	Charity	But deliver us from evil	Gluttony

Prayer

O Father, Giver and Guardian of Peace,
Give me open eyes to see your providence.
Keep gluttony far from my heart. Give me your wisdom.
Never let me become absorbed in myself. Help me to see the needs of those around me.
Come to me, Father, and bless me with greater charity and temperance.
Bring me into your kingdom! Show me happiness.
Through Christ our Lord. Amen.

Three Helpful Truths to Becoming a Peacemaker:

+ The order of life and of creation is given by God's providence.

+ I do not have to invent or redesign God's providential order.

+ My simple task is to seek, know, and faithfully live according to the providence of God.

The Assurance of the Lord Jesus

I have said this to you, that in me you may have peace. In the world you have tribulation; but be of good cheer, I have overcome the world.

John 16:33

The Apostle's Blessing

Now may the Lord of peace himself give you peace at all times in all ways. The Lord be with you all.

2 Thessalonians 3:16

— CHAPTER 8 —

THE PERSECUTED

*Blessed are those who are persecuted
for righteousness' sake, for theirs is the
kingdom of heaven.*

MATTHEW 5:10

The Beauty Remains

While I was a seminarian in Rome, a group of us went to Florence for a vacation over an extended weekend. The city is ornate with beautiful architecture, magnificent statuary, and unparalleled works of painted art. This is the hometown of Michelangelo and Dante, Donatello and Leonardo da Vinci.

On one of the tours of an art gallery, we were told the story of an unknown local artist. Apparently, the man was very skilled and noted for a particular style. With age, however, the hands of the artist became more arthritic and it was difficult for him to paint. He decided to train several disciples in his artistic form. One student singled himself out by his ability to duplicate the teacher's style. Eventually, observers could not distinguish between the teacher and this skilled disciple.

The teacher, however, continued to paint. Tears would roll

down the older man's face as his stiff hands struggled to create the beauty they once did. It took him hours to complete a few strokes of the brush. During this time, the principal disciple cared for his teacher. It hurt him to watch the maestro paint amidst such great suffering.

On one occasion, as the older man was groaning because of the intense throbbing of his hands, the student spoke up. He said to his teacher, "Maestro, you have taught me well. I know your style and it will live on. Please tell me, why are you still painting? You are in such great pain."

The teacher was moved by his student's care and compassion. He sat down, gently smiled, and rubbed his hands. He paused awhile and then said, "I have painted my whole life. My works of art are a reflection of so many experiences and memories." Then, pointing to the various masterpieces hanging on his walls and rubbing his hands again, the artist continued, "And so, even now, I paint. I paint because the pain passes but the beauty remains."

This endearing wisdom is a help to those of us who seek happiness. We must understand that there is more to happiness than euphoria or emotional highs, more than an artificial state of affairs without worry or hassle. Happiness, ironically, requires suffering. We must make the decision to accept the physical, emotional, and spiritual trials God sends us and persevere through them without bitterness. Only then will we find true happiness. And through faith, we know that one day the suffering will fade, but the beauty of the happiness we found through suffering will remain.

The "Seven" Beatitudes

In popular summaries of the Sermon on the Mount, it is generally said that there are eight Beatitudes. There is biblical support for this numbering, but the Christian spiritual tradition has always presented seven Beatitudes since it saw the "eighth beatitude" as more of a commissioning (a call to live them all out) rather than the eighth item in a series.

We enter the kingdom of happiness through the first beatitude: "Blessed are the poor in spirit, for theirs is the kingdom of heaven." Since only the first and eighth beatitude mention "the kingdom," we see the Beatitudes between them as a summary of the dynamics of the kingdom. They are a formation in the kingdom's way of life. Each of them highlights an aspect of Jesus Christ as well as a specific path to happiness.

After being trained in the ways of the kingdom, therefore, we are then called to go out and spread it to others. Since we are in a fallen world that many times favors darkness, bringing the kingdom of happiness to others will bring suffering and persecution. And so the "eighth beatitude" is a summons and a rallying cry to understand and accept persecution for the sake of God's kingdom.

Persecution for the Sake of Righteousness

In life, persecution can be both a blessing and an opportunity.

While not enjoyable or pursued for its own sake, suffering can be a moment of witness and grace to those who do not walk the path of truth and refuse the demands that come with walking that path. In general, attempts to silence, shame, isolate, harm, insult, or slander the one who stands for truth are often derived from a lack of knowledge, a will untrained by virtue, or a misunderstanding of intention. There are times, however, in which persecution is planned and purposely malicious, seeking nothing other than the destruction of goodness and those who seek to share and live by it. In either of the above situations, the one who suffers for righteousness gives witness to the power and eternal nature of truth.

It's worth stressing that in Western societies, the persecuted are not always given physical punishment, as so many in the early Church faced, as well as our Christian brothers and sisters still face today in the Middle East. Sometimes the suffering is social, occupational, economic, or recreational. For example, an employer may refuse to promote an employee because he has publically defended traditional marriage values. And there are so many more issues—protection of unborn persons, the public harm of capital punishment, the proper acknowledgment of two genders, and the preeminence of parental authority—that will not find tolerance but only persecution in many Western societies today.

While the above clarification can help us in our path to happiness, it must still be emphasized that the most fundamental persecution is that which causes death to the witness. Accepting this reality can be a hard thing for the person of good will. In the Christian tradition, such witnesses are called by the set term *martyr*, which is from the Greek word for "witness."

To accept martyrdom requires conviction in moral goodness, courage, trust, and—above all things—the grace of God. Many holy ones have heroically accepted the mantle of martyrdom for the sake of righteousness in service to the common good. Some of these include:

- St. Thomas More for his public opposition to divorce and offenses to religious liberty,
- Blessed Isidore Bakanja for his defense of safe working conditions,
- St. Charles Lwanga and Companions for refusing to perform homosexual acts,
- Blessed Miguel Pro for efforts to minister to those who were ill or suffering,
- St. Jose Sanchez del Rio for teaching others about God and exercising his religious liberty,
- St. Maximilian Kolbe in support of marriage and family life,
- St. Teresa Benedicta of the Cross (Edith Stein) in following her conscience and convictions,
- Blessed Peter To Rot for teaching monogamy and the sacredness of marriage,
- Blessed Joseph Mayr-Nusser in opposition to tyranny and in support of human dignity and civil society,
- Blessed Oscar Romero for speaking on behalf of the voiceless and opposing torture and guerilla tactics against civilians,
- Blessed Miriam Vattalil for advocacy on behalf of the forgotten and landless poor.

The list of holy men and women who made the ultimate sacrifice for the sake of righteousness could go on and on. So many saints have given the human family a powerful witness to truth and goodness in various areas and issues of life.

Our Exemplar and Inspiration

In addition to public witness, the suffering that is accepted for the sake of righteousness can also be an opportunity for the ones who are being persecuted. When suffering is graciously accepted, it can help us to grow closer to God and more deeply understand the Lord's passion, death, and resurrection.

In my own discipleship, I relearned this lesson as a teenager. On one occasion, I stood up for a person with special needs who was being made fun of by some of my friends. None of them enjoyed being called out and quickly turned their jokes against me. I was shocked by their denial of their offense and hurt by the mockery they leveled against me. During my confusion by the whole state of affairs, I bumped into Father Gus, a beloved old Franciscan. He could tell I was upset and asked what was wrong. I started talking, the floodgates opened, and Father Gus just listened. When I was all done, he patted my forearm, hit me with the cincture around his friar's habit, and told me, "Go to the cross and offer it up."

Honestly, I was disappointed by the counsel. I'd heard similar encouragements before but never really understood them. I wanted to say to the good friar, "Listen. This is serious. I need a real solution because I feel really bad right now!" The sentiments must have expressed themselves on my face and demeanor because Father Gus grinned, nodded his head, and continued, "Go to the cross and offer it. Go to the cross . . . because the Jesus you need is nailed to it."

The extended counsel hit my heart like a ton of bricks. It helped me to place my own suffering, a small oblation for the sake of righteousness, within the heart of Jesus and to know that the Lord was with me in my hurt and confusion.

It helped me draw closer to the Lord Jesus and experience a different kind of intimacy with him, and know of his love and saving mission in a radically new way. A treasury of moments like this have helped me understand how *true* happiness and suffering could coexist, and oftentimes do.

It would be helpful here for us to dissect the role of Jesus Christ in his own suffering for the sake of righteousness.

We begin with the truth: Jesus Christ is the Beatitude—the Happiness—of God. He is true God and true man. As such, he is the model of what it means to be human. In his life and saving work, the Lord Jesus showed us how we are to live and how we are to serve others. By understanding the human identity of Jesus, we can see a brighter reflection of our own humanity and can more deeply hear the Lord's teachings.

Christ does not teach us as an outsider but as someone within the human family. In comprehending him in this way, we can comprehend our own dignity and goodness. We realize that we are someone with a unique dimension that is made for happiness, righteousness, and self-donation.

After all the sin and wretchedness we see in our world, it's easy to believe that human beings are evil. Left to itself, such a conclusion about humanity would be understandable (even if wrong). Sin, however, has always been understood as a poverty of being. In seeing that the world and the human person are good and have a natural inclination to goodness (although heavily influenced by an impulse to evil), sin is a privation—a lacking or removal of being—and something that thieves goodness from us, just as darkness is the privation of light and takes away our ability to see.

Therefore, if Jesus Christ was fully human in all things but sin, it reflects the reality that sin is not human or real but is

actually anti-human and anti-reality. Darkness does not have
the power to define humanity, even as it takes away the richness of our human experience and veils goodness from us.

As the exemplar, the "super witness and example," of
humanity, Jesus Christ is without sin and he shows us how
to live as complete human beings. As the Savior of humanity
and the source of reconciliation between God and man, Jesus
Christ takes away the darkness of humanity and allows us to
be happy and free. Pope St. John Paul II would often teach
that we are not the sum of our weaknesses and failures, but
rather the sum of the Father's love for us.

In defeating darkness and sin and experiencing the fullness of human life, Jesus understood and accepted all forms
of suffering. Leading us as the Good Shepherd, he desires to
teach us the scope and purpose of suffering in our lives.

From our fall from grace, suffering is an evil within human
life. It is a consequence of the original sin of Adam and Eve.
In taking on our human nature, the Lord Jesus embraced our
suffering, body and soul. From his life of poverty, to living as a
refugee in a foreign land, to being hunted down as a criminal,
to the frustration of learning a trade, to the death of his foster
father, to his experience of being tired and thirsty, as well as
being misunderstood, rejected, and unloved. All of these sufferings, taken on for the sake of our redemption, culminated
in the cruelty and torture of his passion and the humilia-
tions and asphyxiation of his death. He chose to accept and
use suffering—which has been a pivotal dilemma and source
of anguish throughout human history—as the very means
to manifest his love and restore righteousness to the human
family. And so suffering would become the instrument of our
salvation.

In his mission to take on human suffering, the Lord Jesus went directly to sin, the source of suffering in human life. To take away sin and vanquish its control over humanity, he became sin itself (cf. 2 Cor 5:21). He sought to destroy this privation of being, and its consequences of suffering and death, from the inside out. In becoming sin, Jesus took upon himself all the sins of humanity throughout time. He endured the totality of human guilt, shame, alienation, grief, confusion, and the full panorama of darkness caused by sin.

The crucible for this radically human endeavor was the Lord's passion, which began in the garden of Gethsemane. This was where he took upon the sins of humanity, sweating blood and feeling the full isolation caused by sin, so much that he could not raise his eyes to the heavens (cf. Lk 22:39–46). In this sacrificial moment, the words of the prodigal son could be placed in Jesus's mouth as he suffered in the garden: "Father, I have sinned against heaven and before you; I am no longer worthy to be called your son" (Lk 15:18–19).

The suffering of the righteous was foretold by the prophet Isaiah:

> He was despised and rejected by men;
> a man of sorrows, and acquainted with grief;
> and as one from whom men hide their faces
> he was despised, and we esteemed him not.
> Surely he has borne our griefs and carried our
>   sorrows;
> yet we esteemed him stricken,
> struck down by God, and afflicted.
> But he was wounded for our transgressions,
> he was bruised for our iniquities;
> upon him was the chastisement that made us
>   whole,

and with his stripes we are healed.
All we like sheep have gone astray;
we have turned every one to his own way;
and the Lord has laid on him the iniquity of
us all. (Is 53:3–6)

While the ministry of Jesus Christ destroyed the kingdom of darkness and misery, the consequences of sin still remain in the human experience. The difference, however, is that suffering can now become a source of righteousness for humanity. Rather than seeing suffering in merely negative terms, the example and ministry of Jesus show us a positive way in which suffering can be embraced and become beneficial in life.

And so, will we follow this path of happiness? Will we allow ourselves to suffer for the sake of righteousness and see it as an opportunity to draw closer to Jesus Christ?

The Disciple's Life

As the Lord Jesus suffered for the sake of righteousness, so he calls to each of us: "If any man would come after me, let him deny himself and take up his cross and follow me. For whoever would save his life will lose it, and whoever loses his life for my sake will find it. For what will it profit a man, if he gains the whole world and forfeits his life?" (Mt 16:24–26).

Each of us, therefore, is invited to take up our cross, die to ourselves, and seek righteousness. Jesus has shown us the way in his own path to Calvary, and his apostles, also, serve as great models for righteous suffering, some of whom literally picked up their cross. St. Paul would not be crucified, but he did know a thing or two about suffering. Listen to him describe his many woes:

Are they servants of Christ? I am a better one—I am talking like a madman—with far greater labors, far more imprisonments, with countless beatings, and often near death. Five times I have received at the hands of the Jews the forty lashes less one. Three times I have been beaten with rods; once I was stoned. Three times I have been shipwrecked; a night and a day I have been adrift at sea; on frequent journeys, in danger from rivers, danger from robbers, danger from my own people, danger from Gentiles, danger in the city, danger in the wilderness, danger at sea, danger from false brethren; in toil and hardship, through many a sleepless night, in hunger and thirst, often without food, in cold and exposure. And, apart from other things, there is the daily pressure upon me of my anxiety for all the churches. (2 Cor 11:23–28)

And all that was before he was beheaded! But look at what good came from his many trials. It would do us well to remember this as we face physical illness, financial worries, emotional fatigue, professional stress, and so many other worries. If we are striving to live virtuously and spread God's kingdom, then we can persevere through our labors and know, by the light of faith, that unspeakable good will come from our sufferings.

And so, according to our own state of life, we are each called to stand up for truth, fight for goodness, and defend beauty. The path that allows truth, beauty, and goodness to win is not easy, nor comfortable, but it's worth it as we draw closer to the Lord Jesus.

Our Call and Commission

When Jesus was asked what the greatest commandments were, he gave us two: "You shall love the Lord your God with all your heart, and with all your soul, and with all your mind," and, "You shall love your neighbor as yourself" (Mt 22:36–39). These commandments are the backbone of righteousness. As the Lord would conclude: "On these two commandments depend all the law and all the prophets" (v. 40).

In terms of the first commandment, Pope St. John Paul II teaches us:

> Man cannot live without love. He remains a being that is incomprehensible for himself, his life is senseless, if love is not revealed to him, if he does not encounter love, if he does not experience it and make it his own, if he does not participate intimately in it. . . . The man who wishes to understand himself thoroughly—and not just in accordance with immediate, partial, often superficial, and even illusory standards and measures of his being—he must with his unrest, uncertainty and even his weakness and sinfulness, with his life and death, draw near to Christ. He must, so to speak, enter into him with all his own self, he must "appropriate" and assimilate the whole of the reality of the Incarnation and Redemption in order to find himself. If this profound process takes place within him, he then bears fruit not only of adoration of God but also of deep wonder at himself. (*Redeemer of Man,* no. 10)

The saintly pope's counsel reminds us not to cut short or compromise the work of love and self-donation in our lives.

If we want to know God and ourselves, then we must surrender to Jesus Christ and allow for the appropriation and assimilation of ourselves into his way of life. If the honor due to God's name and glory, or moral truths flowing from his divine law, or religious liberty are attacked, then we are summoned to clarify, defend, and, if necessary, suffer for the sake of righteousness.

This leads us to the second commandment. Again, Pope St. John Paul II reminds us: "A person is an entity of a sort to which the only proper and adequate way to relate is love" (*Love and Responsibility,* Ch. 1).

In an age when the human person is approached so often as a means of pleasure or utility, when so many are convinced that their personhood and dignity (and those of others) are based on what they can accomplish, control, or hoard, we are reminded that as human beings we are worthy of love and respect. Our identity demands reverence and protection from our neighbors and our culture. If this dignity is offended, diminished, or discarded in any way, then we are called to voice concern or opposition, offer fellowship to those in need, stand up for our neighbors and the displaced—whether that's the unborn, the immigrant, the terminally ill, those with special needs, or others—and show a willingness to fight and suffer for the sake of righteousness.

And so our fight and our suffering lead us to be poor in spirit, sorrowful over sin, meek, thirsty and hungry for holiness, merciful, pure of heart, and committed to peace. These are the paths to goodness and holiness, to uprightness of heart and salvation. These are the actions that carry promises which strengthen us as we desire happiness for ourselves and our world. These are the Beatitudes, the avenues that show us the face of Jesus Christ and manifest to us how we are called to live as people destined for happiness.

School of Discipleship

In our School of Discipleship, we have seen a portion of our chart in each description of the different Beatitudes. But now we should look at the chart in its entirety, for it is our road-map to the kingdom of happiness. It gives us a summary of how the Holy Spirit helps us to be happy, how the Lord's Prayer asks for the dispositions we need to pursue happiness, and how the principal Christian virtues maneuver in the wrestling match against the deadly sins that try so hard to destroy us.

BEATITUDE	GIFT OF THE SPIRIT	CORRESPONDING VIRTUE	PETITION OF THE LORD'S PRAYER	CAPITAL SIN/ ANTI-BEATITUDE
Blessed are the poor in spirit, for theirs is the kingdom of heaven	Fear of the Lord	Temperance	Hallowed be thy name	Pride
Blessed are those who mourn, for they shall be comforted	Knowledge	Hope	Thy will be done on earth as it is in heaven	Envy
Blessed are the meek, for they shall inherit the earth	Piety	Justice	Thy kingdom come	Anger
Blessed are those who hunger and thirst for righteous- ness, for they shall be satisfied	Fortitude	Courage	Give us this day our daily bread	Sloth
Blessed are the merciful, for they shall obtain mercy	Counsel	Prudence	And forgive us our trespasses as we forgive those who trespass against us	Greed
Blessed are the pure in heart, for they shall see God	Understanding	Faith	And lead us not into temptation	Lust
Blessed are the peace- makers, for they shall be called sons of God	Wisdom	Charity	But deliver us from evil	Gluttony

Will We Accept the Call?

The Lord Jesus tells us, "As the Father has sent me, even so I send you" (Jn 20:21).

The Lord was sent in poverty of spirit, and so are we. He was a man of sorrows, as are we. The Lord Jesus was meek and we walk with him. He thirsted and hungered for holiness in our world, and we are to have the same yearnings. The Lord was merciful, as we are called to be. He was pure and we are of the same heart. Jesus brought peace and we desire nothing else.

As the Father sent the Lord Jesus, so the Lord sends us!

Based on this solid foundation and united to Jesus Christ, we are challenged to accept the Great Commission. "All authority in heaven and on earth has been given to me. Go therefore and make disciples of all nations, baptizing them in the name of the Father and of the Son and of the Holy Spirit, teaching them to observe all that I have commanded you; and behold, I am with you always, to the close of the age" (Mt 28:18–20).

The kingdom of happiness is ours . . . it's yours! And it needs you to take it into the whole world. And so say a prayer, put this book down, be happy, and go spread his kingdom!

Prayer

All-powerful Father,
You sent us your Son, your Happiness;
help me to live with him so that I may be happy.
Open my heart and show me your loving kindness.
Keep misery and darkness far from me.
Come to me, Father, and bless me with your beatitude.
Bring me into your kingdom! Show me happiness.
Through Christ our Lord. Amen.

Three Helpful Truths to Suffering for Righteousness:

+ I am weak but greatly loved by God.
+ God desires that I be an instrument of his goodness in our world.
+ I can rely on God's strength to speak, act, and suffer for righteousness.

Encouragement of the Lord Jesus

And do not fear those who kill the body but cannot kill the soul; rather fear him who can destroy both soul and body in hell. Are not two sparrows sold for a penny? And not one of them will fall to the ground without your Father's will. But even the hairs of your head are all numbered. Fear not, therefore; you are of more value than many sparrows.

Matthew 10:28–31

A Reflection of the Glory

Then one of the elders addressed me, saying, "Who are these, clothed in white robes, and from where have they come? I said to him, "Sir, you know." And he said to me, "These are they who have come out of the great tribulation; they have washed their robes and made them white in the blood of the Lamb. Therefore are they before the throne of God, and serve him day and night within his temple; and he who sits upon the throne will shelter them with his presence. They shall hunger no more, neither thirst any more; the sun shall not strike them, nor any scorching heat. For the Lamb in the midst of the throne will be their shepherd, and he will guide them to springs of living water; and God will wipe away every tear from their eyes."

Revelation 7:13–17

BIBLIOGRAPHY

General References:

Pope John Paul II. Encyclical *Redemptor hominis* (1979).

—————. Encyclical *Veritatis Splendor* (1993).

Theme-Based References:

Aquinas, Thomas. *Treatise on Happiness. Summa Theologica,* I-II, Q. 1-21. Translated by John Oesterle. Notre Dame: University Press, 1984.

Ashley, Benedict. *Thomas Aquinas: The Gifts of the Spirit.* New York: New City Press, 1995.

Cantalamessa, Raniero. *Beatitudes: Eight Steps to Happiness.* Cincinnati: Servant Press, 2009.

—————. *Poverty.* New York: Alba House, 2005.

Chaput, Charles. *Strangers in a Strange Land.* New York: Henry Holt, 2017.

Cook, Jeff. *The Deadly Sins and the Beatitudes: Recovery and the Seven Deadly Sins.* Grand Rapids: Zondervan, 2008.

Garrigou-Lagrange, Reginald. *Beatitude.* London: Aeterna Press, 2016.

Groeschel, Benedict. *Living the Beatitudes: Heaven in Our Hands.* Cincinnati: Servant Press, 1994.

Konyndyk DeYoung, Rebecca. *Glittering Vices.* Grand Rapids: Brazos Press, 2009.

MacArthur, John. *The Beatitudes: The Only Way to Happiness.* Chicago: Moody Publishers, 1998.

Pinckaers, Servais. *The Pursuit of Happiness—God's Way.* New York: Alba House, 1998.

Ratzinger, Joseph. *Jesus of Nazareth: From the Baptism in the Jordan to the Transfiguration.* New York: Doubleday, 2007.

Sheen, Fulton. *The Cross and the Beatitudes.* Tacoma: Angelico Press, 2012.

———. *The Seven Capital Sins.* New York: Alba House, 2012.

Tomlin, Graham. *The Seven Deadly Sins.* Oxford: Lion Hudson, 2007.

Vogt, Emmerich. *The Freedom to Love.* Minneapolis: Mill City Press, 2012.

Wiersbe, Warren. *Heirs of the King: Living the Beatitudes.* Grand Rapids: Discovery House Publishers, 2007.

Wojtyla, Karol. *Love and Responsibility.* San Francisco: Ignatius Press, 1993.